COVENANT • BIBLE • STUDIES

The Chronicler

Robert W. Neff
Frank Ramirez

faithQuest® ♦ Brethren Press®

The Chronicler
Covenant Bible Studies Series

© 2010 *faithQuest*®. Published by Brethren Press®, 1451 Dundee Avenue, Elgin, IL 60120. For publishing information, visit www.brethrenpress.com.

All rights reserved. No portion of this book may be reproduced in any form or by any process or technique without the written consent of the publisher, except for brief quotations embodied in critical articles or reviews.

Unless otherwise noted, scripture quotations are from the New Revised Standard Version of the Bible, © 1989 National Council of the Churches of Christ in the United States of America. Used by permission. All rights reserved.

Cover photo © 2010 Beverly Vogel. Used by permission.

Library of Congress Cataloging-in-Publication Data

Neff, Robert W.
    The chronicler / Robert W. Neff and Frank Ramirez.
        p. cm. — (Covenant Bible studies series)
    Summary: "Provides Bible study on 1 and 2 Chronicles for use in a small group setting"—Provided by publisher.
    Includes bibliographical references (p.   ).
    ISBN 978-0-87178-132-1
    1. Bible. O.T. Chronicles—Textbooks. I. Ramirez, Frank, 1954- II. Title.

BS1345.55.N44 2010
222'.6007--dc22

                          2010008000

14 13 12 11 10   1 2 3 4 5

Manufactured in the United States of America

To our colleagues at Bethany Theological Seminary, 1965–1979, who with us shared an alternative Anabaptist and Pietist way of following the gospel of Jesus Christ.

Contents

Foreword

The Covenant Bible Studies series provides *relational* Bible studies for people who want to study the Bible in small groups rather than alone.

Relational Bible study is marked by certain characteristics that differ from other types of Bible study. We are reminded that relational Bible study is anchored in covenantal history. God covenanted with people in Old Testament history, established a new covenant in Jesus Christ, and covenants with the church today. Thus, this Bible study is intended for small groups of people who can meet face-to-face on a regular basis and share frankly and covenant with one another in an intimate group.

Relational Bible study takes seriously a corporate faith. As each person contributes to study, prayer, and work, the group becomes the real body of Christ. Each one's contribution is needed and important. "For just as the body in one and has many members, and all the members of the body, though many, are one body, so it is with Christ. . . . Now you are the body of Christ and individually members of it" (1 Cor. 12:12, 27).

Relational Bible study helps both individuals and the group claim the promise of the Spirit and the working of the Spirit. As one person testified, "In our commitment to one another and in our sharing, something happened. . . . We were woven together in love by the Master Weaver. It is something that can happen only when two or three or seven are gathered in God's name, and we know the promise of God's presence in our lives."

In a small group environment, members aid one another in seeking to become

- biblically informed so they better understand the revelation of God;
- globally aware so they know themselves to be better connected with all of God's world;

- relationally sensitive to God, self, and others.

For people who choose to use this study in a small group, the following intentions will help create an atmosphere in which support will grow and faith will deepen.

1. As a small group of learners, we gather around God's word to discern its meaning for today.
2. The words, stories, and admonitions we find in scripture come alive for today, challenging and renewing us.
3. All people are learners and all are leaders.
4. Each person will contribute to the study, sharing the meaning found in the scripture and helping bring meaning to others.
5. We recognize each other's vulnerability as we share out of our own experience, and in sharing we learn to trust others and to be trustworthy.

The questions in the "Suggestions for Sharing and Prayer" section are intended for use in the hour preceding the Bible study to foster intimacy in the covenant group and to relate personal sharing to the Bible study topic, preparing one another to go out again in all directions to be in the world.

Welcome to this study. As you search the scriptures, may you also search yourself. May God's voice and guidance and the love and encouragement of brothers and sisters in Christ challenge you to live more fully the abundant life God promises.

Preface

There is more than one way to look at a historical event, no matter how clearly established the facts. That came home to me when I left Interstate 70 at Frederick, Maryland, and visited the Monocacy National Battlefield. In response, I wrote an article called, "The most important battle you've never heard of."

On July 9, 1864, Confederate General Jubal Early's seasoned forces defeated inexperienced Union troops commanded by Lew Wallace (who would later write *Ben Hur*). There are several monuments raised by the Daughters of the Confederacy commemorating the victory. But there are also many monuments celebrating the *Union* victory—for in winning the battle the Confederates were delayed a precious day, preventing them from marching into an undefended Washington, D.C., before reinforcements arrived. There is obviously more than one way to look at that battle.

There is also more than one way to look at a biblical event, no matter how inspired the account. In *Side by Side*, an earlier Covenant Bible Study, I explored scriptures with such contrasting viewpoints they almost seemed contradictory. More recently, the two present authors wrote *Country Seer, City Prophet*, another Covenant Bible Study that examined key events in sacred history from the contrasting viewpoints of two prophets, Isaiah and Micah, who lived through the same events but saw them through the lenses of their different backgrounds.

So, what does this have to do with Kings and Chronicles? On more than one occasion I have led study groups through the entire Bible over the course of one year. There were generally two complaints. First of all, Leviticus is *way* too long. The second was that folks had the feeling that in Chronicles they were just reading the same stuff they'd already encountered in Kings.

In this study, author and scholar Bob Neff demonstrates several ways in which the Chronicler (the author of 1 and 2

Chronicles) tells the same story we read in 1 and 2 Kings, but from a different viewpoint and with a different interpretation. Both accounts are recognized as inspired by God's people, and both are included in the collection of Hebrew Scriptures. The study questions are designed to help you and your group wrestle with these differences, as was no doubt intended by the ancient rabbis who included both in the canon.

Just as this study will talk about the Chronicler's narrative as an alternate history, the guiding materials for sharing and prayer will also explore an alternate and ancient approach to the faith: Celtic Christianity. The Celtic civilization stretched across northern Europe all the way to the British Isles. The Celts did not recognize a sharp division between the sacred and the secular, nor between the divine world and the earthly world we inhabit. Roman Christians cherished stories of survival against harsh odds—Jonah, Daniel in the lion's den, and the three young men in the fiery furnace—but Celtic art depicted stories of Jesus healing and inserted the life-giving cross into the circle, their symbol of the life-giving sun. (For more on this, see *Irish Jesus, Roman Jesus* by New Testament scholar Graydon F. Snyder.)

While some may find the idea that there is more than one way to view the biblical narrative *within* the Bible strange, most everyone would agree there is more than one way to approach God in prayer. Celtic Christianity provides one vibrant and living way to approach God. If you buy, borrow, or download a good book on Celtic prayer you will discover there are prayers for justice and prayers for sleep, prayers for mercy and prayers for milking, prayers for traveling and prayers for plucking wool. Celtic prayer draws in all of life's experiences and all of creation into a universal prayer of praise to God, and invites God into every aspect of life with vibrant, homey language. There is no aspect of life too extraordinary or too ordinary to be the subject of prayer. Every aspect of life is related to God. Conversation between earth and heaven covers the great and small, the mundane and magnificent.

In each prayer session we will focus on one section of the Celtic prayer known as the Lorica (the Gaelic word is often translated as Breastplate) of St. Patrick, and in the final session we will pray the entire prayer as a whole. This prayer encompasses all of life's experiences, weaving the seen and the unseen into one confession of faith to provide protection and security. This particular translation is by Cecil Frances Alexander, who authored many hymns, including "All things bright and beautiful," "There is a green hill far away," "Jesus calls us," and "Once in David's Royal City." Her translation of St. Patrick's Breastplate may be found in the back of the book, starting on page 77.

As in the three previous guides we co-authored, after meeting together to talk through the subject the two of us mapped out this study book together, although unlike before it took a different course as we wrote. Bob is the brains behind this partnership; he is responsible for the scholarship and wrote the first drafts of each chapter. I am the brawns, having learned ten-finger typing in the seventh grade. On receiving each chapter I responded with suggestions for rewrites, primarily with clarity in mind. Bob did the rewrites, after which I contributed items for Personal Preparation, Suggestions for Sharing and Prayer, and Discussion and Action.

Frank Ramirez
Everett, Pennsylvania

1

What If?

Personal Preparation

1. Write a one-sentence description of what it means to be a follower of Jesus on a piece of paper. Fold it over, tape it shut, and bring it to the session.
2. Take time to pray through the Breastplate of St. Patrick. A translation of this Irish prayer is provided at the back of the book, or you may find a different translation in another book or on the Internet.
3. Look up a short introduction to 1 and 2 Chronicles in a study Bible or in a commentary, Bible dictionary, or Internet article.

Suggestions for Sharing and Prayer

1. Whether yours is a new group or a group that has met many times in the past, it is always good to continue to learn more about one another. Invite each person to make a one-sentence statement about him- or herself. When all have shared, invite group members to take turns lifting up a sentence prayer for another person in the group, based on that person's sharing. At the end of each sentence prayer the group may respond in unison: "Lord, hear our prayer." Conclude with the Lord's Prayer.
2. Turn to the Breastplate of St. Patrick printed at the back of the book. The prayer is often divided into nine different sections. The opening sections list those things claimed by the one praying as part of divine protection

from God against the ills and temptations of the world. Just as this study focuses on differing ways of telling Bible history, the first section of this prayer centers around the Trinity—three different ways we know the one God.

3. The leader may pray the first section of this prayer aloud, slowly. Pause, and then invite everyone to pray this section in unison. Pause, and encourage anyone who wishes to select one word or phrase and pray extemporaneously on that word or phrase. At a point that seems appropriate, the leader may conclude with his or her own prayer.

4. Consider the following questions: Do we all experience God in the same way? How have group members experienced or known God? What is your understanding of what it means to be "Three in One and One in Three"? What does it mean to bind or claim the "strong Name of the Trinity"? How comfortable are you with ambiguity in your relationship with God? How is your relationship with God different than your relationship with people?

5. Pray the first section of the prayer once more in unison.

Understanding

I had a difficult time getting started on this project. I spent most of the spring stewing over how and where to begin. Then in June the latest *Star Trek* movie was released. While I am not a Trekkie, I went to see it. Without going into great detail, the movie is about the destruction of Vulcan by a Romulan general who blames Spock, a Vulcan, for the loss of his own home. The Romulan general seeks not only to destroy Vulcan but all the major planets in the galaxy, including Earth. The destruction of Earth is avoided by an alternative story that happens through a level of time warping that lies outside my scientific imagination. Nonetheless, this movie creates a story line in which a whole new history of the Enterprise emerges that I am sure will lead to a new round of *Star Trek* movies. These sequels will follow an alternative path, a different history to the one we already know. There will be a whole other way of looking at *Star Trek* history.

At about the same time as I saw this movie, I came upon a book by Diana Butler Bass entitled, *A People's History of Christianity: The Other Side of the Story*. On the inside of the dust jacket are these words, "For too long, the history of Christianity has been told as the triumph of orthodox doctrine imposed through power and hierarchy." In *A People's History of Christianity*, Butler Bass reveals an alternative history and argues that this other side of history "is not a modern phenomenon, but has always been practiced within the church." Another alternative story was staring me in the face, which appeals to my Anabaptist way of looking at the world. As part of the left wing of the Reformation we have always argued that the true church was corrupted by Constantine, and because of him the real history of the church disappeared. I've always had a different way of looking at Christian history.

Every Picture Tells a Story
Now, how do all these observations relate to the book of Chronicles? Maybe one way to answer this question is to figure out how Chronicles defines itself. The title for the book comes from Jerome, who in the fourth Christian century described the book as *chronikon*, a word for history. This book, a single narrative divided into two volumes in Christian Bibles, is indeed a history. In her commentary on this book, Sara Japhet observes that the Hebrew title of Chronicles, *dibre hayammim*, is best translated as "The Events of the Days." This really describes its genre, namely history (1). Rabbinic tradition designates the book, "The Book of Genealogies," in large measure due to its inclusion of genealogical detail. The Septuagint—the Greek translation of the scripture made for Jews who could no longer read Hebrew—called it *paraleipomena*, which means "the book of the things omitted" or "left over" (1).

The Greek translators rightly observed something crucial that is often overlooked: this book is a different way of looking at the history of Israel. It is an alternative history that does not focus on the same details as the previous canonical works. This other way of looking at sacred history is why the author of Chronicles, who is often called the Chronicler, felt the need to tell this story when we already had a history of God's people in Samuel and Kings.

That's because the Chronicler, who probably composed his work sometime in the fourth century BCE, lived in a different time and circumstance than the earlier biblical historian.

The Chronicler not only had the first four books of the Bible (Genesis to Numbers) to work with, he also had what is called the Deuteronomistic history (Deuteronomy through 2 Kings), which was fundamentally complete and available. In commenting on the style of the Chronicler, Japhet observes that the Chronicler is characterized by "the combination of faithful adherence to his sources with freedom to change" (41). The Chronicler accepted the earlier sources, but wrote an alternative history that would inform contemporary life from a different perspective on the past. Why did the Chronicler write in this way?

Never Was Always Been

In *Reading Utopia in Chronicles*, Steven Schweitzer, dean and professor of Old Testament studies at Bethany Theological Seminary, draws a distinction between the two meanings of utopia. One comes from the Greek *outopia*, meaning a place that does not exist, and the other from *eutopia*, meaning a better place. Thomas More's *Utopia*, for instance, defines a better place and demonstrates a better way to live and act in what is an imaginative place. These utopian works live in the tension between what is fantastic and impossible and what is visionary, and in Schweitzer's words, "better-than-the present, and an alternative reality" (15). The writer of Chronicles creates an alternative story that does not ask us to live in some fanciful, never-never land, but in the present. By writing an alternative history, the Chronicler paves the way for renewal and refinement of life in his own community.

Steven Schweitzer maintains that the book of Chronicles was written with a view that this is the way history should have been—errors of the past are erased, royal leaders become just and inclusive, and Judah's history provides devotional innovation and intensity. This alternative history provides an alternative way to behave in the present. Unlike past interpreters, he suggests that this alternative history provides an avenue for renewal and reawakening in a difficult and bleak period. Chronicles provides a fresh approach for looking at our past and learning from it.

So why do we need an alternative history? Because in life, as well as in the Bible, there is always a legitimate and alternative way of looking at things. Both Matthew and Luke, for example, build their Gospels around the life of Jesus. But Matthew wishes to demonstrate to an audience familiar with the faith history of the Bible that Jesus fulfills the Hebrews scriptures, while Luke demonstrates to the Roman Empire that the life of Jesus and the spread of Christianity bring salvation to all without threat to the Roman order.

One final illustration that has become a part of our contemporary culture may assist us in our understanding. Think of Dr. Seuss' story, *How The Grinch Stole Christmas!* The Grinch shares the modern misconception that Christmas is about getting as much stuff as one can. When he steals all the gifts for the children of Whoville, the Grinch expects that the spirit of Christmas will be destroyed. To his surprise, on Christmas morning the same joy abounds in the village below. The joy of the day destroys the Grinch's intent. The Grinch discovers that Christmas "means a little bit more." We don't know where Whoville is, but we know that it exists wherever this day is celebrated. The true intent of Christmas is recovered by an alternative story that embodies the real meaning of this celebration.

As we begin this study, we will find that a book often neglected because of a basic misunderstanding of what it purports to do may become an example of the way we ought to examine our own story and our place within it. Hopefully we will also discover the vibrant nature of Scripture, which invites us to playful engagement with a text that brings us to a new sense of God's way with humans.

Discussion and Action

1. Have you ever heard a sermon on 1 or 2 Chronicles? If so,

what was it about? Under what circumstances have you read these books? What is your impression of Chronicles compared to 1 and 2 Samuel and 1 and 2 Kings?

2. Name one important event from the distant past. Then name one important event from the more recent past. Discuss what happened and how important the event was. What are the alternative views or versions of these stories? What informs your way of looking at events such as these?

3. Talk about different ways of looking at your own life story. What different interpretations could you make about the way things have turned out? Which interpretation do you choose, and why? What one event, if changed, might have made everything turn out differently? Do you think it would have been for the better or for the worse?

4. Collect group members' descriptions of what it means to follow Jesus (see "Personal Preparation"), and then pass them out randomly. Read them aloud, one by one. How similar are they? How different? How important are the differences?

5. Neff suggests that there are two distinct ways of looking at history in the Old Testament—through the eyes of the Deuteronomist and through the eyes of the Chronicler. Were you aware of these two histories? What does Neff say the Chronicler is trying to do? Why is Chronicles necessary?

6. How does our view of history affect our future together? Is an "alternative history" simply another way of looking at things? Is it deceptive? Is it truthful? Discuss your responses.

7. What is the difference between a different way of looking at things, and a different way of believing? Is it possible for people of the same faith to have differing viewpoints? Explain your responses.

8. The chapter talks about creating a utopia in our minds. Is this simply wishful thinking, or does it encourage us to create a better world? Should a Christian, by believing in

a better place or by believing we are called to create a better place, make things happen, or should Christians wait for things to happen? How does a utopia help us, like Chronicles, to discover the real meaning of what has and will happen?

2

The Legacies of Family
1 Chronicles 1–9

Personal Preparation

1. Read 1 Chronicles 1–9. This is largely genealogy. Underline, if you choose, names in the genealogy that you recognize. Allow your mind to wander into prayer and speculation as you read. Are there ways of reciting the genealogies to make them fun?
2. Put together your own faith genealogy. Who do you consider your ancestors in the faith? To whom are you directly related? Which individuals, movements, or denominations are "cousins" to you? Are there religious forbears you are embarrassed to have in your genealogy?

Suggestions for Sharing and Prayer

1. Gather together and share high points of the past week. If some in the group have experienced the same events on a personal or societal level, reflect briefly on similar or varying viewpoints of these events. Draw these reflections together in an opening prayer.
2. Spread out a sheet of newsprint or make available a large drawing surface. Invite one person to read aloud the second part of the Breastplate of St. Patrick. Invite others to draw simple representations of the sequence of events described in this section.
3. Patrick claims events from the life of Jesus "by power of faith" as protection. There are many alternative ways

to tell the story of Jesus. Brethren theologian Dale Brown once commented that his complaint about the classic creeds of the church is that they jump from the birth of Jesus to the death and resurrection without mentioning things like the Sermon on the Mount and his other teachings. Reflect on your experience of Jesus and tell your own story of Jesus after the manner of this prayer. Write out these versions on more newsprint, and illustrate them in the same manner.

4. Gather together and pray, first using Patrick's words, then the words of all the alternative stories of Jesus. Conclude with the words of Jesus by praying the Lord's Prayer in unison.

Understanding

I am prone to run right through the genealogical material in the Old Testament. However, thanks to an incident that occurred this past summer, I have a new appreciation for 1 Chronicles 1–9.

The organizers of a Martin family reunion decided to invite the maternal side of the family, the Heinaman clan. Thomas Heinaman, a minister in the Christian and Missionary Alliance church who is also a genealogist, has traced this side of our family back to the Revolutionary War and beyond.

Most of our family lineage includes Mennonite and Brethren stock of a peace-loving kind, but it turns out we have an exception—an exceptional Lutheran warrior. One of our forbears was a Hessian soldier captured at the Battle of Trenton in 1776 and brought to Lancaster County as a prisoner of war. When the war was over, he married a girl named Maria. It's said that Hessian mercenaries were constantly drunk, which is supposedly why so many were taken prisoner. Thomas, however, maintained that our distant relative was sober, like so many other Hessian foot soldiers who were frightened for their lives since they were so distant from the British base camps. It was the officers who were drunk.

Genealogies are often filled with surprises: some we may wish to bury, others we may wish to polish up a bit, and others we may wish to highlight. The Bible's genealogies are no different.

Bigger Surprises

The Chronicler relies heavily on Genesis, and in the first nine chapters provides us with a quick thumbnail sketch of the continuous line of humanity from creation until the time of Abraham and beyond to the exile. Why include such a long and boring section? First of all, it's not boring if it is your family, and this is, after all, our spiritual family.

One reason for the genealogy, which I believe was written in a time of distress, is to remind us that humanity can survive even the direst of circumstances. However, the real goal is stated in chapter 2: "These are the sons of Israel: Reuben, Simeon, Levi, Judah, Issachar, Zebulun, Dan, Joseph, Benjamin, Naphtali, Gad, and Asher" (1 Chron. 2:1-2). This founding family is crucial to the Chronicler's understanding of history.

We might expect that the eldest son would be treated first, but this is where the surprise comes in. The writer makes it clear that Reuben forfeited his birthright by "defiling his father's bed" (5:1) in an adulterous relationship with his father's concubine. The birthright is inherited by Joseph, the beloved of his father according to biblical tradition. But the really important patriarch is Judah, one of the younger sons. The Chronicler uses history to explain why Judah's and Levi's families are so important, while others have disappeared altogether. Even though Joseph is the hero of the Genesis saga and his lineage is extended by his two sons, Manasseh and Ephraim, they are accorded little more than half a chapter. Only a few verses are devoted to Naphtali, none to Dan and Zebulun. This lack of attention may reflect the loss of records about these tribes when their territory was swallowed up by Assyria in the eighth century BCE, or maybe just the shifting character of the family of Israel.

Judah's elevation (2:3) is not due solely to the role of Judah himself, but to the fact that the monarchy, especially David and Solomon, springs from his branch of the family tree. The third chapter, the pivot of the genealogy contained in chapters 2–9, is crucial for the Chronicler. The descendents of David and Solomon are the focal point of the genealogy because they are the focal point of the history of Israel.

Just as Thomas Heinaman made my genealogy come alive by connecting the present with the past, the Chronicler makes the biblical genealogy compelling by connecting the distant past with the time of his first readers. He does this through Anani (3:24), who is also mentioned outside the Bible in a letter from Elephantine (407 BCE): ". . . his colleague the priests in Jerusalem and to Ostanes, the brother of Anani and the nobles in Jerusalem" (Pritchard 492).

Another striking development is the inclusion of non-Israelite groups and tribes in the family history. First Chronicles 4:13 mentions the sons of Kenaz; Numbers 32:12 identifies Caleb as a Kenizzite. This is as surprising as the discovery of a Hessian soldier in my Brethren and Mennonite ancestry. Caleb and Joshua were the only wilderness wanderers who followed the Lord without reserve. While some tribes disappeared from view, others experienced greater integration in the family tree because they embodied the devotion to God that is critical to the writer in his retelling the story of Israel.

Look Back to See Forward

The Chronicler uses genealogies to justify the triumph of kings from a less likely family and to highlight the significance of programs that they established. The Levitical (or priestly) functions that persisted into the period of the Chronicler—which was after the people had returned from exile in Babylon and were living once more in the Promised Land—can be traced back to the time of Moses. The allocation of the lands assigned to the Levites in Joshua became a function of the king in the time of the united monarchy under David (see Joshua 21:42). The Levite genealogy in chapter 6 underscores the importance of David in the establishment of the temple singers—even before the temple was built—and the worship associated with them. In the Palestinian canon (one of the orders in which the books of the Bible were copied in the ancient world), Chronicles precedes the Psalter because of its interest in the character of worship practices in the temple.

The conclusion of the genealogy begins: "So all Israel was enrolled by genealogies; and these are written in the Book of the Kings of Israel. And Judah was taken into exile in Babylon because of their unfaithfulness. Now the first to live again in their possessions in their towns were Israelites, priests, Levites, and temple servants" (9:1-2). After a brief overview of those who returned (9:3-9), the attention returns to the Chronicler's primary concern: the continuation of the worship life of Israel. First to be mentioned are the priestly families, and then the Levitical families (9:10-16). As in the past, these families will again take charge of Israel's worship life. In the description of the gatekeepers (9:17-32), it is clear that they continue the function of those who earlier worked with the tabernacle. They care for the utensils used in the service; they rise early in the morning to open the sanctuary; they stay close at night to protect it; and they polish the furniture. Their office of trust goes back to Samuel and David (9:22).

Now we are in a position to understand the genealogical introduction to the book. The writer maintains that through the centuries there has been continuity of service to God. What better way to demonstrate that than through the continuity of families and their responsibilities. The temple programs, instituted by David six hundred years earlier, are still intact. From my wife Dottie, who taught in Franklin Park, Illinois, the industrial center of Chicago, I learned that the children of immigrants could often trace their family tree back generations to a little village in Italy or a small town in Eastern Europe. Sociologists tell us that people who have experienced displacement depend upon genealogies and family associations as a source of comfort. The genealogical introduction to Chronicles offers comfort and assurance that the story will go on with its principal center—the life of devotion located in the temple at Jerusalem—intact.

Genealogies tell us not only who we are, but how we want to be perceived. As people of faith, Chronicles is about our family. So it's important for us to sort out our place in this story, too.

Discussion and Action

1. Discuss the biblical genealogy in 1 Chronicles 1–9. Which of these persons would you want as part of your genealogy? Which would you rather not claim?

2. Neff tells how there was a surprise in his genealogy. What do you know about your ancestry? What surprises have you discovered in your story? How does that inform your self-image? Why do some people like to take credit for things done by their ancestors? How valid, in your opinion, is this attitude?

3. What would the genealogy of your congregation look like? How far back does it go? Is it a story of faithfulness? How many people are involved? What are the surprises in your congregation's past?

4. How is the story of your community told? Consider checking to see if there are monuments or plaques that might need some restoration, or if there a need to institute such memorials in your community.

5. Many of us skim over the genealogies of 1 Chronicles 1–9. You might think, "If it is not my family, why should I care?" What reasons does Neff give for us to care? What are some important reasons for reading and studying the biblical genealogy? Which, if any, do you think are important?

6. Through the person of Anani, the Chronicler connects the ancient past with his present. How do you and/or your church view your connection with the ancient past? Where does Bible history touch your congregation's life? What connections, if any, do you feel with scripture that make it your story?

7. Neff states that "another striking development is the inclusion of non-Israelite groups and tribes in the family history." How well does your church do in incorporating new names and new families into its fabric? Is there resistance to new people?

8. Neff talks about "continuity of service to God" as a key point to the Chronicler's genealogy. To what extent are

you part of a "continuity of service"? Where do you fit in? How do you perceive yourselves as individuals and as a church? How do others perceive you? How do you want to be perceived?

3

The Prayer of Jabez
1 Chronicles 4:9-10

Personal Preparation

1. Read 1 Chronicles 4:9-10, which is presented in the back of this book in more than one translation. Write or print the Prayer of Jabez in the translation you prefer most (from the back of the book or elsewhere) and take it along to Sharing and Prayer. Also, make a list of points the prayer centers around.

2. Make a list of the "landmarks" of your faith—those events, those people (known to you personally or through their writings or reputation) whose lives have been an inspiration to you, and those portions of the Bible that are important to you. Bring this list to Sharing and Prayer.

Suggestions for Sharing and Prayer

1. Greet one another by passing the peace of Christ. One person begins, "The peace of the blessed Lord be yours," and another responds, "We share this selfsame peace." Let everyone greet each other in this manner. Take time to share the events of the past week. Lift up concerns in prayer.

2. Gather in a circle. Invite a volunteer to recite the third section of the Prayer of St. Patrick. Others may pray it as they choose, in its entirety or particular lines that have meaning for them. This portion of the prayer ties together "landmarks" of faith—both from the unseen world,

such as angels, and from words and actions in faith history. (The phrase "purity of virgin souls" seems to refer to the actions of the righteous, not to a particular person in biblical history.)

3. Discuss which elements of the prayer are meaningful to you, and those portions with which you may not feel such a strong connection.

4. Refer to the lists of "landmarks" of faith—those events, people, scriptures, and readings—that have been meaningful to members of the group. Restate the third portion of the Prayer of St. Patrick using your lists. If they wish, group members may explain the reasons for their particular choices. Pray your landmarks together as a group.

5. This week's session centers around a different kind of prayer, a petitionary prayer that makes specific requests of God. Known as the Prayer of Jabez, it is found in 1 Chronicles 4:10. Take a few minutes to compare the prayer in your various translations. Discuss what you mean by petitionary prayer and what you consider an appropriate petition directed to God. Conclude the session by praying the Prayer of Jabez together, using your different translations simultaneously.

Understanding

I first heard of the Prayer of Jabez almost a decade ago when Bruce Wilkinson wrote a best seller by that name. *The Prayer of Jabez* is a small book, 4 by 6 inches, with only eighty pages of text. The prayer itself is only one verse long: "Oh that you would bless me and enlarge my border, and that your hand might be with me, and that you would keep me from hurt and harm!" (1 Chron. 4:10). Wilkinson argues that this little-known Bible hero could be the answer to releasing God's power and favor in one's life, and suggests that devout individuals should make it a daily prayer to break through to a new life with God. He has gone all over the country lecturing about *The Prayer of Jabez* and hearing the testimonies of thousands of believers who say that it has changed their lives. That's a lot of mileage out of one verse.

At first glance, the prayer seems out of place. Everything around it is genealogy. Genealogies are filled with names and those names have meaning, but explanations for those names are more often found in birth narratives, such as with the birth of Isaac. Sarah exclaims that everyone who hears of a birth at her age will laugh (Gen. 21:6). The Hebrew word for laugh is *tsachaq*, from which we get the Hebrew name *yitschaq*, which in English is Isaac. That response of joy is what we often encounter, even after the difficult pains that accompany labor and birth.

In contrast to Sarah, the mother of Jabez thinks only of the pain her child has brought her. We don't know whether it was a difficult pregnancy or a difficult labor and birth. In any event, she reflects on the curse that falls upon women in Gen. 3:16*b*, "in pain (*'etseb*) you shall bring forth children." Hebrew is a language built around three consonant roots. In this case the words for pain (*'etseb*) and Jabez (*'ebets*) share the same three consonants, though in a different order. The name is understood as "the one who brings pain." What a way to saddle a child with a great burden!

What's in a Name?

In Hebrew thought, names not only carried a sense of reality, they were that reality. Think of Samuel and his story in the book named for him. In Hebrew his name means "God hears," which describes the prophetic message he brings. Then think of Jabez and the talk his name must have evoked. "Oh look, here comes the one who brings pain." It's hard to shake a name like that!

Unlike Job and Jeremiah, Jabez does not curse the day of his birth or the parents who brought him into this world. He doesn't ask for a change of name. He calls on God. There is an interesting play here on the Hebrew word for call (*qara'*). Despite the fact that his mother *called* him a name with negative connotations, Jabez *calls* on God in a positive fashion. The same word is used in both instances with a dramatic change in effect. Calling on God trumps the overwhelming reality of the name-calling.

Jabez lives within the context that has been determined for him. However, he makes an appeal to a higher authority and asks God to bless him and enlarge his territory. He does not assess blame for his circumstance, but asks God to help him make the most of it. In her commentary on Chronicles, Sara Japhet asserts that Jabez takes the only step possible: "God's power alone is superior to and more effective than the potency of the name, and it may be acknowledged in prayer." The power of the name is "not denied, but it is subordinated to the mightier power of God" (110). Jabez lives in the belief that he may appeal to God and find a way through difficult and otherwise defining moments. He believes God will assist in defining his life. Neither his name nor the circumstances of his birth will define who he is. God's blessing will.

Some individuals must confront barriers such as handicaps, place of birth, unaccepting parents, or economic dislocation. These circumstances define a different starting line for these individuals. One reaction is to complain and do nothing about it. Another is to rise above it by seeking a different way. Jabez is an illustration of the second type of person who intends to change his difficult circumstance.

Abide with Me
In the second part of the prayer, Jabez asks for God's hand to be upon him, indicating that Jabez does not want to plot his own direction but wants to follow God's guidance. The prayer not only asks for assistance in the immediate circumstance, but in the future as well. In this second part of the prayer there is a request for God's continuing guidance. Wilkinson prays this prayer every day as a way of pursuing God's guidance in each moment of his life.

For the third part of the prayer, I favor the NKJV translation: "And that You would keep me from evil, that I may not cause pain." The first half of this section sounds much like the Lord's Prayer, "lead us not into temptation, but deliver us from evil" (Matt. 6:13, KJV). Jabez asks God to keep him out of harm's way so that he may escape events and circumstances that will cause him harm. His request turns from guidance to protection.

Similarly, I begin every day asking for God's protection with the words of St. Patrick. Patrick was confronted with enemies who sought his life, and in anticipation of that ambush he asked God to shield him and provide him with protection in a beautiful prayer that begins, "For my shield this day, I call a mighty Power . . . ."

The NKJV translation rests on a technical grammatical reading, which comes down to the difference between reading a pronominal suffix as subject or object of the verb. The NRSV uses the latter reading. In contrast, Wilkinson uses the pronominal suffix as subject. Though his name reminds everyone that he brought pain to his mother, Jabez asks that he may cause no one pain. This request turns the whole passage on its head; the one who through no fault of his own caused pain in childbirth now asks that he avoid causing pain or harm to others throughout his life. A remarkable request!

This small passage is bounded by two observations. The first is that Jabez was honored more than his brothers. The word *kabad* (to honor) is the same as the one used in the Ten Commandments where we are called to honor father and mother. The one dishonored by his name is now honored by the quality of his life over against his kinsman. In this list of outstanding representatives of Judah, a man of simple faith is elevated by the simplicity of a prayer.

The second observation forms the other boundary to this vignette: "And God granted what he asked." God answered Jabez's prayer. In the midst of the long pedigree of the tribes of Israel and their significant members, we are again reminded of what really matters to the Chronicler—the life of devotion.

Discussion and Action

1. Jabez carries a great weight in his name that could have prevented him from reaching his full potential. What barriers, handicaps, and other "different" starting lines have you experienced or observed in others. What effect has that had in your and their accomplishments?

2. The name "Jabez" carries negative connotations. Isaac's parents waited a long time for his birth and experienced a good deal of trouble and trial, but his name is "laughter." Birth stories generally involve some level of pain (as well as humor, tragedy, triumph, etc.). What is the story behind your birth? Why were you given your name? What effect has your name had on your life?

3. What effect can negative words have on a child or an adult? What should a person do to overcome negativity? To what extent do words *reflect* reality or *create* reality?

4. What do you think Jabez means when he asks God to enlarge his territory? Is this simply about physical boundaries? What events in your life have expanded your territory or horizons? How does one go about transcending limitations experienced earlier in life?

5. Look at the various translations of the prayer of Jabez at the back of this book. Note how differently the last phrase is treated. Talk about the difference in meaning between "that I may not cause pain" (NKJV) and "that you would keep me from hurt and harm" (NRSV).

6. The text states that God granted what Jabez asked. In what ways has God answered your prayers? Is prayer "successful" or "unsuccessful" depending on God's answer?

7. Neff compares this prayer to the prayer of St. Patrick, which calls upon God to act as a shield. What sort of protection do you need or require? How have you acted as a shield of protection for others?

8. Do you generally pray the same words, or do you pray with different words and thoughts? Why do you think certain sorts of prayers suit you best? What place does devotion and prayer play in your life? How is your prayer life organized and planned?

9. The scripture states that Jabez received more honor than his brothers. How do you define honor? What does it mean to honor someone, and what does it mean to receive honor? What place does honor have in your view of life?

4

The Other David

Personal Preparation

1. Read 2 Samuel 6:16, 20-23 and 1 Chronicles 15:27-29 together. Note similarities and differences in a notebook or by writing directly on the text. Take your notes along to the group session.
2. Think of a hymn that celebrates the wonders of God's creation. If possible, take a copy of it with you to the group session. Also, make a note of a place or aspect of creation in which you take strength and comfort. Write down what, where, and why. If possible, find a photograph to take with you to the group session.

Suggestions for Sharing and Prayer

1. Greet one another and share news of the past week. Offer sentence prayers about concerns and joys that are shared. Then share favorite hymns about nature, such as "Morning has broken" and "How great thou art." Close with a reading of Psalm 8.
2. Share your notes or photos about a place or aspect of creation in which you take strength and comfort. Let members reflect on places that are special, telling their personal history with that place along with the reason for the attachment. Note those places that are close at hand and those that group members have visited rarely, once, or simply imagined. Discuss the extent to which group members believe God is revealed in creation.

3. Today's fourth portion of the Breastplate of St. Patrick involves claiming the wonders of creation as part of God's divine protection. Invite a group member to recite one line of this prayer, and then pass it along to the next person to read a line. Continue until the entire section has been read aloud. Next, pray the prayer together in unison. Then, once again take turns reading the section line by line, pausing after each line to allow group members to pray about that line, enriching the images with further description based on personal observation and experience. For instance, in praising God for "the virtues of the star-lit heaven," group members might express thanks for especially dark nights when the stars are clearer, or about specific stars that have meaning for a person, or aspects of stars someone may have discovered in personal reading.

4. Return one more time to this stanza of the Breastplate of St. Patrick, inviting group members to add lines reflecting places special to them.

5. Close by choosing one of the hymns from earlier in the session and singing it.

Understanding

Some historians believe that an American president's real place in history cannot be determined until decades after leaving office. Should their legacies be defined primarily by their accomplishments, or should everything be included in determining their significance? For example, should Bill Clinton be judged on balancing the budget, bringing peace to the Balkans, or by his personal indiscretions? Is Jimmy Carter to be judged on his four years as president or his decades as an ambassador for peace? Do we remember Franklin Roosevelt for programs that restored jobs and dignity to the destitute or for signing the order to intern Japanese-Americans during World War II?

The Chronicler made his judgments, not decades, but centuries later. The Chronicler sees what remains of the reign of David after five hundred years have elapsed. This perspective informs what he includes in determining David's legacy.

Remember, the Chronicler provides an alternative view of history. In contrast to the story of David in 1 and 2 Samuel, the Chronicler omits some key issues, embellishes others, and creates variations on the older story. What results is an idealized version of David's life. The Chronicler doesn't just want to make David look good; he also wants to assist later readers in understanding the key contributions this king made to the life of Israel.

One of the Chronicler's biggest omissions is the story of David's adultery with Bathsheba, the murder of Uriah the Hittite, and the consequences of David's sin on his reign (see 2 Samuel 11–19). Samuel focuses on sexual improprieties in the king's household, including the rape of Tamar by her half-brother Amnon and the rebellion of Absalom. These episodes are all missing from Chronicles. The Chronicler seems to maintain a view of the universe in which one gets what one deserves: the righteous are rewarded and the wicked are punished. Yet in spite of this strong moral cast to his work, he is more concerned about personal relationships to God than what we might call personal sins.

An incident about Michal, Saul's daughter, is symptomatic of his dynasty's lack of concern for the ark and other religious traditions. When David returns to the palace after bringing the ark of the Lord to Jerusalem, he is quite extravagant in his celebration. Michal accuses him of vulgarity in his ecstatic display of devotion: "How the king of Israel honored himself today, uncovering himself today before the eyes of his servants' maids, as any vulgar fellow might shamelessly uncover himself!" David responds by saying, "It was before the LORD, who chose me . . . as prince over . . . the people of the LORD, that I have danced before the LORD" (2 Samuel 6:20-21). Clearly the concern in this passage is David's deportment and the rift it creates between Michal and the king.

Listen to this same scene from Chronicles: "David wore a linen ephod. So all Israel brought up the ark of the covenant of the LORD with shouting. . . . As the ark of the covenant of the LORD came to the city of David, Michal daughter of Saul looked out of the window, and saw King David leaping and dancing; and she despised him in her heart" (1 Chron. 15:27c-29).

The character of David's devotion is in play in each incident, but the rationale for Michal's reaction changes significantly. In 1 Samuel, it appears to be his naked exposure before the ark. In Chronicles, David seems to be fully clothed; her displeasure comes about because of his devotion to the Lord of Israel. In the instance of Bathsheba, the Chronicler omits whole sections of material; in the relationship with Michal he edits the material to describe David's complete devotion to God.

When We Get to Jerusalem

In the next example, the bringing of the ark to Jerusalem, the Chronicler adds verses to demonstrate David's style of leadership: "David consulted with the commanders of the thousands and of the hundreds, with every leader. David said to the whole assembly of Israel, 'If it seems good to you, and if it is the will of the LORD our God, let us send abroad to our kindred . . . including the priests and Levites . . . that they may come together to us. Then let us bring again the ark of our God to us; for we did not turn to it in the days of Saul.' The whole assembly agreed to do so, for the thing pleased all the people. So David assembled all Israel . . . to bring the ark of God from Kiriath-jearim" (1 Chron. 13:1-5). These five verses were composed by the Chronicler to demonstrate several dimensions of David's kingship.

In the first place, David consults with those who are around him and asks the people whether this action seems good to them. Japhet makes the following observation: "According to 2 Samuel 6, the transfer of the ark is essentially David's decision. The focus of the story is David: his actions, feelings and words. According to the Chronicler's introduction, only the idea and the initiative are David's, while the actual decision is to be taken by the people as a whole. In Chronicles there is a changing attitude toward the people's role in the political life of Israel *vis a vis* the king. . . . The people are not limited to playing the role of accompanying crowd . . . ; rather they are full partners—in consultation and decision making" (274). The people are involved in the devotional life of Israel and fully participate in its direction.

This is evident in the Chronicler's accounts of the dedication of the temple (2 Chron. 7:8) and the Passover of Hezekiah (2 Chron. 30:5). David's insistence on inclusion is emphasized again when the ark finally rests at its place in Jerusalem. The Chronicler observes that "he distributed to every person in Israel—man and woman alike—to each a loaf of bread, a portion of meat, and a cake of raisins" (1 Chron. 16:3). What a remarkable sense of inclusion in an assembly normally restricted to men. The author makes it clear that "everyone" means both genders.

An Inconvenient Truth

In this recounting of the ark's return, the writer deliberately ignores a dark moment in the life of Israel: the capture of the ark by the Philistines. A more complete version of the story can be found in 1 Samuel 4–6, which describes the failures of Samuel's sons at the sanctuary where the ark was kept, leading to the capture of the ark by the Philistines. David's commitment to the ark sustains continuity with Israel's past—the ark is the artifact of the religion of Moses.

As we have seen, the Chronicler ignored, refurbished, or edited whole segments of the earlier history to fit a particular view of history, a view that emphasizes the involvement of the people in decision making, the complete devotion of David to his Lord in contrast to the disobedience of Saul, and the inclusiveness of the community of faith. Bringing the ark to Jerusalem illustrates the continuity of faith from the time of Moses to the present. Describing the loss of the ark would have detracted from that purpose.

Discussion and Action

1. The opening paragraph invites us to consider how politicians should be remembered. Discuss what a legacy means. Should personal mistakes outweigh accomplishments, or even be mentioned? Discuss what you would like to be remembered for, and what you wish others might forget.

2. Neff notes that the Chronicler makes no mention of David's adultery with Bathsheba. If you attended Sunday school as a child, do you recall any lessons that dealt with this aspect of his reign? If not, what was mentioned? What did you hear from the pulpit about David? How did this change as you became an adult? If David's sins were part of the story that you heard, what difference did it make?

3. Consider ways in which the group can support the preservation or restoration of God's creation. Is there the possibility of tree planting, park maintenance, or animal advocacy?

4. What are some differences between the way the story of David and Michal is told in 2 Samuel and 1 Chronicles? What difference does the material missing from the Chronicler's account make? Discuss whether the Chronicler's choice to emphasize some material and eliminate other material is legitimate. What does this say about how you view any dialogue within scripture?

5. According to Neff, the Chronicler attributes a collaborative style of leadership to David. What is your experience when it comes to leadership in church? Is collaboration the norm or an anomaly? Which sort of leadership do you favor?

6. What does Neff conclude about the effect of and reason for the Chronicler's editorial changes? When you retell stories from your life, do you delete facts that do not seem pertinent to you? Share some examples.

7. Christians speak of being saved by grace, not by works. If this is true, why is it important to consider another's deeds at all? Is the real measure of a person not what they believe, but what they do? When you attend a funeral, do you expect the eulogy to stick to the good associated with the deceased? Are you alarmed if there is focus on the faults of the deceased?

5

An Editor's Selection that Leads to Praise

Personal Preparation

1. Read 2 Samuel 6:17-19 and 1 Chronicles 16. Also read Psalms 96; 105:1-15; and 106:1, 47-48, which are part of the soundtrack of the Chronicler's account. Make notes about a special event at your church and how it may have been seen differently by different people. What happened? Was there a meal, music, worship, play?

2. Sharing and Prayer will include singing "I bind unto myself today," a musical setting for the Breastplate of St. Patrick. Find a copy of this song to practice. If it is not familiar, listen to it at www.cyberhymnal.org.

Suggestions for Sharing and Prayer

1. Greet each other with words of praise. Gather around a television and play a short movie clip that features no dialogue but has a thrilling soundtrack. Turn off the sound and play the scene again. What difference do you notice? How essential is the music to the scene?

2. In 1 Chronicles 16, the writer includes a "soundtrack" for the installation of the ark of the covenant in Jerusalem. Discuss what place music has in the worship life of your congregation. In your opinion, is this a satisfying place? Is there a danger of taking music for granted? Explain.

3. This week's fifth section of the Breastplate of St. Patrick calls upon the reader to rely on God for personal attention and protection. The assumption, common in Celtic prayer, is that God is not a spectator but an active participant in history. Read this section of the prayer together. Though you may not conceive of God literally having eyes, ears, and hands, discuss how these images might strengthen the idea of God's close presence.

4. The translation printed in this book was set to music for *The Irish Hymnal.* It is a beautiful tune that requires work. Find a copy of the music and sing the hymn all the way through. (If you are using *Hymnal: A Worship Book*, it is hymn No. 441.) Note that this setting doesn't include all the stanzas in Alexander's translation, but they could be added.

5. Take time now to share some of the joys and concerns of the past week, lifting them up in sentence prayers. Conclude by singing "Joy to the world," a hymn based on Psalm 96, one of those sung in the Chronicler's account.

Understanding

When I began to ponder the way 1 Chronicles was put together, I couldn't help but think of American composer Charles Ives' work, *Three Places in New England.* Ives combined fragments of marches, popular tunes, and hymns from the American past and arranged them in entirely new ways for a rather striking musical outcome. In turn, this made me think of the difficult—and invisible—work of a film editor.

No matter how perfect a film might seem, be assured that it is the result of a good deal of editing. Editors make hard choices. They have to select a few scenes out of many to get the message across. A lot of great stuff is left on the cutting room floor. That's why it's great when an editor has the chance to reinsert scenes that were cut or to introduce an alternate ending on the DVD. For example, the *Blade Runner* DVD was issued with *five* different versions. You could almost have a totally different film!

In a way, this is how the Chronicler worked. He had almost the whole Hebrew Bible to work with, so he could choose what he wanted to share of the past. Although the Deuteronomist and the Chronicler tell the same story, the way they edited their materials almost makes it feel like we're at different movies. Chapter 16 is a perfect example.

The Chronicler splits 2 Samuel 6:17-20a into two parts, with 1 Chronicles 16:1-3 being parallel to 2 Samuel 6:17-19a, and 1 Chronicles 16:43 being parallel to 2 Samuel 6:19b-20a. The passage about Michal and her response to David has been moved to a time prior to the ark's arrival in Jerusalem. The arrival of the ark is no longer blemished by a marital spat or any untoward act. The conclusion is now marked by the departure of the people and David's blessing of his home, which now leads into God's blessing of him by Nathan in 1 Chronicles 17.

What's most important for the Chronicler is what happens between these two parts. In the 2 Samuel version of the arrival of the ark, the people eat and then leave for home immediately (2 Samuel 6:19). By the lengthy intrusion of forty verses in Chronicles, we get an entirely different view of what happened. In this insertion, the Chronicler tells us about the installation of various Levitical priests to minister before the ark (vv. 4-7 and 37-42), and Asaph and his brothers sing a conglomeration of psalms taken from the fourth collection in the Psalter.

However, what is more important to note is that the people are now engaged in full-fledged praise of God: "Then all the people said 'Amen!' and praised the LORD" (v. 36b). The people express their devotion to God in hymns of praise. The focus is no longer on a free meal but in an engaged devotional life. As I was writing this section, I thought of our own love feast. As communion ends, we sing a hymn and depart for our homes. However, the focal point of this event—as with the passage in Chronicles—is praise of God.

Words and Music

How is this new hymn organized? Not very unlike the narrative structure of this chapter! Psalms 105 and 106 are separated by Psalm 96, to which we will return in a moment. The hymn begins in 1 Chronicles 16:8 with the first fifteen verses of Psalm 105, which celebrate God's guidance of the patriarchs. The citation ends before the time of Joseph and Moses described in the rest of this psalm. The patriarchs become elevated by their being called prophets and anointed ones (Psalm 105:15); the second title is usually reserved only for kings. They were few in number and they wandered over the world, but God protected them, even rebuked kings on their account (1 Chron. 16:19-22). By making the editorial decision to edit Psalm 105 in this way, the Chronicler has, according to Roddy Braun, permitted these "verses to stand as a timeless principle, applicable in his own day: *It is the people Israel, reduced in number and without a homeland which is protected by God.*" To a people whose recent recollection is deportation and exile, these are comforting words.

Interestingly enough, the Chronicler uses only three verses from Psalm 106: the first line and the last two. The final verse is the conclusion of Book Four (Psalms 90–106) of the Psalter (there are five books in all), and calls for the people to say "Amen" and "Praise the Lord!" This admonition is now recorded as the response of the people in Chronicles. The writer appeals to this psalm because of its affirmation that God's *chesed* (steadfast love) endures forever, an affirmation made in the psalm in spite of the people's rebellion at every turn. The Chronicler simply eliminates the verses of Psalm 106 that recount the past iniquities of the ancestors. The Chronicler focuses on God alone. I don't think the Chronicler intended to soft pedal these past sins as much as to take the attention off of the past and direct it solely to God, which is what these cited verses do.

In verses 23-33, the Chronicler recites almost all of Psalm 96, which is one of my favorite psalms and is the basis for the Advent carol, "Joy to the world." Why is this psalm the center of the attention in this chapter? The answer is simple. This psalm centers on praise to God, who is above all other gods in the universe. There are a whole series of imperatives for the worshiper: sing, declare his glory, ascribe to the Lord, worship, and be in awe. The worshiper is bathed in praise and thanksgiving because of the overwhelming power and majesty of the God of Israel. There is little change in the citation of this psalm because I believe the Chronicler believed it said all that needed to be said.

Soundtrack Available at all Fine Stores
The Chronicler took the edited film and added a soundtrack. A good soundtrack is crucial because without music a film can fall flat. The best are almost invisible. These psalms of praise are the essential soundtrack for setting the mood the Chronicler wishes to create. Including songs helps this passage tell a vividly different story. When a film has a great soundtrack, we take the film with us; we hum the tune or sing the words. God's people don't want this wonderful occasion to end, and their soundtrack probably continued to ring in their ears.

Praise is the focal point of this chapter, because praise takes us outside of ourselves. As a worshiper, the more we direct our attention to God, the more we forget about ourselves—our distractions, our anxieties, and our misfortunes. We become energized because of the larger perspective that praise grants us: it ushers us into the universe where heaven and earth rejoice and where trees jump up and down in joy. It's hard to avoid laughing and shouting uncontrollably in this world of praise. It demands trumpets, drums, and cymbals. In these moments, the world is transformed and we enter the alternative universe that the Chronicler wants to portray. It is at this point that we can understand the purpose of the Chronicler: that God should become all in all.

Discussion and Action
1. Consider the two retellings of an important event in the life of God's people. Which sounds more exciting? In

which would you have preferred to participate? Which
sounds more like the worship in your congregation?

2. What part does music play in your worship? Who par-
   ticipates? How are the various generations involved? Do
   all people generally feel comfortable taking part in the
   music ministries of the church? What goes on among
   congregants during preludes and postludes?

3. What, to you, has been the most memorable musical
   moment in your congregation? What event might have
   been improved by music?

4. What is your favorite hymn? What is your least favorite
   hymn? What styles of music do you prefer, and at which
   sorts of events? Which musical genres do you consider
   inappropriate for worship?

5. Consider having a mini hymn sing. Close with "Joy to
   the world," which is based on Psalm 96, one of the
   psalms sung in 1 Chronicles 16.

6. When you think back on scenes from your life, do you
   sometimes edit your memories? Why? Have you ever
   listened to someone's story about your shared past and
   realized they have edited, subconsciously or otherwise,
   their memory of the event? What events from your life
   do you wish you *could* edit?

7. Compare and contrast 1 Chronicles 16 and 2 Samuel
   6:17-19. Recognizing that both versions of this celebration can be true, what is the result of the Chronicler's
   editing of the Deuteronomist's earlier account? What is
   the function of the Psalms in the Chronicler's account?

8. How worried do people seem about the length of worship services at your church? Do they linger, or do they
   rush in and out? What is your own arrival and departure
   habit?

9. Neff translates the Hebrew word *chesed* as "steadfast
   love." In light of what is described as God's affirmation
   despite "the people's rebellion at every turn of their history," what can be assumed regarding God's steadfast
   love? While most agree that it is important to study and

know the past to avoid repeating mistakes, what can be the benefit of looking beyond the past to the present relationship with God?

10. How is this account made richer by the Chronicler's addition of what Neff describes as a "soundtrack"? What would praise and worship be like without music?

6

The Promise to David

Personal Preparation

1. Read 2 Samuel 7:1-17 and 1 Chronicles 17:1-15 side by side, verse by verse, charting differences and similarities.
2. Reflect on promises made by you and to you. How many of these promises have been kept? How many have been broken? What was the nature of the commitment made by you or to you?
3. The leader should prepare a receptacle to receive slips of paper in which they can be safely burned.

Suggestions for Sharing and Prayer

1. Greet one another with words of peace and faith. Share current concerns and joys. Draw these together in a prayer.
2. Reflect on the dangers, snares, and temptations for which you crave strength and/or protection. Share with each other only to the level that you feel comfortable; silence can be strengthening. Allow group time for silent reflection on difficulties, shared or borne alone.
3. Pass out slips of paper and pencils to each person, asking each to write down a besetting sin, temptation, or obstacle. Emphasize that these will shortly be destroyed and that no one will read them. Fold the slip in half and then in half again. Slips may be taped shut if that increases the feeling of security. Hold on to the slips.

4. Celtic prayer recognizes that the world is essentially
    wonderful, but that the misuse of that which is intrinsi-
    cally good can be a temptation or snare. The sixth por-
    tion of the Breastplate of St. Patrick focuses on sin, vice,
    lusts, and hostile persons, which can be a roadblock to a
    godly life. Allow a long pause for silent reflection after
    each line, as one person reads this portion of the prayer
    aloud. When time has passed, the leader may prompt the
    group as a whole to respond in unison, "God who pro-
    tects, God who preserves, hear our prayer."
5. Invite group members to place their slips of paper into the
    receptacle. Use a match to set them ablaze in a safe man-
    ner. As they are reduced to ash, sing "Amazing grace"
    together.
6. Spend some time sharing about individuals who have
    been a source of strength and inspiration. Share as well
    those things of the earth—objects, places, living or oth-
    erwise—from which you draw strength. How important
    is it to know that one is not alone when facing the diffi-
    culties of life?
7. Close by reciting this week's stanza together, conclud-
    ing with the Lord's Prayer.

Understanding

Abraham Lincoln may have been the greatest president ever, but
during his lifetime people saw him in radically different ways.
This was made clear in a political cartoon. On the left panel,
Lincoln is portrayed as the goddess of peace. On the right, he is
dressed as Mars, the god of war. People saw him both ways.

Both 2 Samuel 7:1-17 and 1 Chronicles 17:1-15 depict King
David after north and south have been united under his rule and
the ark of the covenant has returned to the tabernacle. Like
Lincoln, one account appears to see David as a man of peace and
the other as a man of war.

The Old Testament centers on a series of covenants with
individuals and the people of Israel. These promises are the driving force in the course of history—the covenant with Noah that

promises that God will never send a flood again (Gen. 9), the covenant with Abraham that promises the giving of the land and numerous descendents (Gen. 17), and the covenant at Sinai with the giving of the law (Exodus 19–24 and Deuteronomy). The first two are unconditional promises, but the covenant at Sinai is conditional and persists only as long as the people obey. By the time of the monarchy, the covenant came to rest on the king.

This led to a fourth covenant. In 2 Samuel 7, the prophet Nathan shares God's promise with David: "Your house and your kingdom shall be made sure forever before me; your throne shall be established forever" (v. 16). This promise is unconditional and remains at the heart of both Jewish and Christian thought. It is repeated in its entirety in 1 Chronicles 17, though with differences that reflect the specific concerns of the Deuteronomist and those of the Chronicler.

To begin with, the phrase in 2 Samuel 7:1, "the LORD had given him rest from all his enemies," is simply eliminated in 1 Chronicles 17. Why? Because in the Chronicler's view, David has not yet completed his nation building. In 1 Chronicles 18–20, David is still waging war with the Moabites, Ammonites, Arameans, Edomites, and Philistines. For the Chronicler, David is a man of war and has the responsibility of securing the nation against its external enemies. He has not completed this at the time of Nathan's promise, and thus the nation is not at rest.

This Old House

Secondly, Chronicles notes that the ark of the covenant will dwell in a tent while David is returning to his house of cedar. This observation leads David to propose something better for God's dwelling. He shares this desire with Nathan, who assumes that it is a good idea. Unlike 2 Samuel, where the response is a bit more diplomatic, in Chronicles Nathan immediately reports that God has rejected David's offer categorically (1 Chron. 17:4). Reading between the lines, God is putting David in his place. God will be the one who makes the plans. It reminds me of God's response in Exodus 3 when Moses asks for God's name, and God answers, "I AM WHO I AM." God tells Moses to back off and not try to control the relationship. For the Chronicler, it's less about David and more about God.

God reminds David that this need for a house was never a desire from on high. It was God who made David ruler over Israel, defeated his enemies, and established *his* preeminent reputation throughout the world (vv. 6-10). Then God turns the tables on David by promising to build his house (his descendents). The same word (*bayit*) in Hebrew is used for house (a building) or a household (line of descendents). God has completely taken the initiative out of David's hands. God doesn't deny the need for a permanent dwelling, but David will not be the one to build it. This will only occur after God has established David's house.

There are striking differences between Samuel and Chronicles regarding the conclusion of this promise. 2 Samuel 7:14 holds out the possibility of punishment for a disobedient king; no such disobedience is foreseen in Chronicles so this reference is dropped. In both accounts there is no threat to the household, as appeared in the case of Saul. There is also a shift in the framework around the promise. In Samuel it is David's house, David's kingdom, and David's throne that will last forever. But the Chronicler, writing centuries later, knows that there is no longer a descendant of David on the throne.

This helps explain the way these affirmations are made in Chronicles: "I will confirm him in my house and in my kingdom forever" (7:14). The Davidic king is God's vice-regent on earth—he is part of God's kingdom, not the other way around. This theme is precisely what is represented in the Psalms quoted in the previous chapter of Chronicles. God's universal reign is celebrated in the fourth collection of the Psalter (Psalms 90–106), not that of the Davidic line.

This universal reign embraces all empires and all times, so that even with the destruction of Jerusalem, God's reign continues. Babylon is not in charge, God is. Even though the thread of the Davidic line appears to disappear for a while, the expectation is that this line will be restored. As we can see in the New Testament, Jesus fulfills this promise to David.

Next!

In both accounts, God establishes who will succeed David (1 Chron. 17:11; 2 Samuel 7:12). The Chronicler asserts that the dynasty encompasses both David and Solomon, which accounts for the enhanced role he gives to Solomon. Commenting on verse 14, Japhet observes: "The present verse reflects this new outlook: not David's day, indeed, but the combined reign of David and Solomon constitutes the climax of Israel's history, and it is in Solomon that the promise is fulfilled" (335).

David's response to Nathan's vision is a contrite prayer: "Who am I, O LORD God, and what is my house, that you have brought me thus far?" (1 Chron. 17:16). Note how often God is called upon as either Lord, Lord God, or God. David is in a state of high agitation and solemnity, underscoring the great distance between David and God. This is a prayer of reconciliation, since David's mood is one of "complete resignation to the will of God, accepting with equanimity both the refusal of his original wish and the promise of what he did not ask" (the promise of a house; Japhet 336).

Verses 20-22 highlight the theme of the Psalms alluded to above—there is no God like you, who creates a people through great and terrible events, redeeming them from Egypt and driving out all nations before them to make them your people. Then in the concluding verses (vv. 23-27), David returns to the promise that his house will be established forever. He ends with a request: "Therefore may it please you to bless the house of your servant, that it may continue forever before you" (v. 27). In these six verses, David refers to himself as servant six different times, continuing in the spirit of contrition with which he began.

This passage, whether from 2 Samuel 7 or 1 Chronicles 17, is crucial for all messianic thought. In the words of Roddy Braun, "From this time forward it will be impossible for the Messiah to be considered anything less than David's descendent, and when messianic thoughts are expressed, it will be most commonly in terms related to David and his family" (209). Thus, the New Testament begins with Matthew 1 tracing the lineage of David:

"An account of the genealogy of Jesus, the Messiah, the son of David."

Discussion and Action

1. Name the different covenants mentioned in this chapter and whether they are conditional or unconditional. Which covenants or relationships in your life are unconditional? Which are conditional?

2. Discuss any significant differences you found in the two accounts. Is it possible for two people at the same event to come away with the same impressions? Why, or why not?

3. What were David's reasons for wanting to build a house for the ark of the covenant? How would building a temple have made David look in the eyes of others?

4. The prophet Nathan initially tells David to go ahead, but returns later to state otherwise. When politicians change their minds they are sometimes accused of "waffling" by their political opponents. What effect does this have, do you think, on people examining issues with honesty and changing their minds when they believe they have been incorrect?

5. Neff notes that "God is putting David in his place." It's not about David. It's about God. One often hears people talk about "my God" and "my Bible" as if they belonged to them, instead of them belonging to God. What other phrases, attitudes, or actions suggest we are confused about who is in charge?

6. Why did the Deuteronomist see David as a man of peace, while the Chronicler viewed him as a man of war? How can these two viewpoints be reconciled? Might both be true? What does this suggest when individuals or countries view the same events in radically different lights?

7. How would you describe King David's response to the message from God? Do you view this reaction in a positive or a negative light? What disappointments have you

endured? Have you ever changed your plans in response? If so, what unexpected new opportunities opened up?

8. The Deuteronomist and the Chronicler were writing in different times. How did this affect their interpretations of the promise to David regarding the throne and his line? What does this change mean for Christian interpretation of this promise?

9. Jesus is described as a descendant of King David. We think of Jesus as the embodiment of God's kingdom, which is supposed to endure forever. Which resonates more with you—Jesus as son of David or as Son of God?

7

David—The Careful Planner

Personal Preparation

1. Read 1 Kings 1–2 and 1 Chronicles 28–29. Consider what it means to plan for the future. What sort of future would you like to leave behind for those who come after you? Have you made plans? What are they?
2. On a piece of paper, write down one hymn you would like sung at your funeral, one scripture you would like read, and three things you would like said about your life. Bring your list along to the group session.

Suggestions for Sharing and Prayer

1. Arrange seating so that group members do not face each other, but instead face forward, as if in a chapel. Play gentle and quiet music in the background as people arrive. Once all have arrived, invite group members to treat this opening as a memorial for everyone in attendance. Invite people, one by one, to rise and say something true and good about someone else in the group, making sure each person is spoken about in this way. Sing a stanza of a favorite hymn to close this section.
2. Now rearrange seating in a circle facing one another. Share the lists group members created regarding hymns, scriptures, and stories you would like shared at your funeral. Reflect on the planning you have done for the future, and your connection to that future and those whom you love who may be a part of that future. Close with extemporaneous prayers for each other.

3. The seventh stanza of the Breastplate of St. Patrick invokes the protection of Christ against a wide range of dangers. Invite one person to pray this stanza aloud. Define how you might interpret each line. For instance, what constitutes "false words of heresy" or "heart's idolatry," and what sort of protection might be needed? Make notes, so that when finished the group may pray their own version of this stanza. Pray the two versions together, alternating the two first lines, the two second lines, etc., pausing between each couplet to allow time for reflection on the meaning.

4. As you close, reflect on what lies ahead for each individual this coming week. Pair off and pray one for the other for blessings and the protection of Christ in the week ahead.

Understanding

The United States was traumatized in 1963 when John F. Kennedy was assassinated and in 1974 when Richard M. Nixon resigned in disgrace, but in both instances there was no insecurity about the succession of the vice president to the presidency.

That wasn't the case in 1841 when William Henry Harrison became the first president to die in office. Some believed that John Tyler would only be the acting president and that true power would lie with the cabinet. By his actions, Tyler established the precedent we rely on today for the smooth transition of power.

However, in nations where there is no clear succession or where succession can be bypassed by chicanery and political maneuvering, there is a great deal of dread and insecurity. Consider the amount of discussion regarding succession in countries like North Korea or Cuba.

After a long and successful reign, King David approaches the end of his life and the matter of succession becomes crucial. As in the case of other passages, the Deuteronomist and the Chronicler take a good hard look at what happened when King David died. They see things quite differently.

Up to now there has been a close relationship between the Chronicler's portrayal of David and the material in 1 and 2 Samuel. However, in 1 Chronicles 22–29, which describes the transfer of power from David to Solomon, there are only a few verses drawn from this source.

Some interpreters suggest that the Chronicler carefully studied the sections of Deuteronomy and Joshua about the transfer of power from Moses to Joshua and crafted a history that complies with what he found there. Such a view would explain a major break with Kings in which the Chronicler suggests that the transfer of power passed smoothly from David to his son Solomon.

By contrast, succession is under dispute in the Deuteronomist's version. In the last chapters of 2 Samuel and 1 Kings 1–2, David is portrayed as growing so weak that he needs a nurse to assist him. Palace intrigue enables Adonijah to be crowned king, only to have key personnel intervene (with the help of Bathsheba) to secure the throne for Solomon.

Everything Shipshape

In Chronicles, David himself secures the throne for Solomon: "When David was old and full of days, he made his son Solomon king over Israel" (1 Chron. 23:1). David is active right up until the end. This sounds a lot like the description of Moses, who was full of spit and vinegar right up to the day of his death (Deut. 34:7).

Another similarity is that both Moses and David are cursed with fatal flaws that keep them from fulfilling their mission. Moses is kept from entering the Promised Land because he acted inappropriately by striking the rock at Meribah and Massah in anger (Deut. 3:26*ff.*). David is unable to build the temple because he has "shed much blood and . . . waged great wars" (1 Chron. 22:8). Yet David was fighting these wars to secure the land for the people of God. The Chronicler applies a theological principle that goes deeper into the very character of temple building by drawing on verses like 1 Kings 6:7, which states that no tool of iron was heard in the temple while it was being built, and Exodus 20:25, which says that stones hewn with a sword are not to be used in building an altar to God. Japhet, a noted commentator on Chronicles, concludes: "The clear statement that use of force is incompatible with the building of altar or temple is the Chronicler's main theological contribution" (397).

The peaceful character of Solomon, both in the significance of his name and in the absence of warfare during his reign, underscores the belief that the temple must be built by a man of peace. Notice the following: "See, a son shall be born to you; he shall be a man of peace. I will give him peace from all his enemies on every side; for his name shall be Solomon (*shelomoh* from the Hebrew word for *shalom*), and I will give peace and quiet to Israel in his days" (1 Chron. 22:9).

Japhet suggests the postponement in building the temple arises out of historical necessity (396). As a man of war, David may be prevented from building the temple, but according to the Chronicler, he lays the groundwork for it to be accomplished after he is gone.

David then encourages Solomon: "Now, my son, the LORD be with you, so that you may succeed in the building the house of the LORD your God. . . . Be strong and of good courage. Do not be afraid or dismayed" (1 Chron. 22:11, 13). This encouragement is intended to assist Solomon in completing the task. It recollects when Moses told Joshua to be strong and bold, so that he might bring the people into the Promised Land (Deut. 31:23; Joshua 1:6).

Lasting Legacy
Both Moses and David have major disappointment in their lives—neither fulfills a lifelong dream. Yet each fulfills his commitment to the next generation, reaching the final stage of development in Erik Erikson's (an internationally recognized developmental psychiatrist) chart of the mature life. Such attitudes enable succeeding generations to stand on the shoulders of their forebears and achieve more than they could have otherwise dreamed.

Because of Solomon's inexperience and the importance of the task that lies ahead (1 Chron. 22:5), David makes preparations for the building of the temple. He first gathers materials in great quantity—stores of iron for nails, bronze for overlay, and huge quantities of cedar (1 Chron. 22:2*ff.*). Secondly, he establishes the location for the temple (1 Chron. 21:28*ff.*). Thirdly, he organizes the Levites and the priests (1 Chron. 24–25) and makes provision for the temple musicians, gatekeepers, and other officials (1 Chron. 26).

Such planning is the work of a mature individual. This concern for the future contrasts with some modern attitudes as found in the bumper sticker often plastered on the back of an RV: "We're spending our kids' inheritance." One also encounters this attitude in some older adults who dismiss global warming and suggest that it doesn't really matter what happens to the environment after they are gone.

After making these arrangements, David gives Solomon his plans for the temple, the divisions of the priests and Levites, and the vessels of the temple (1 Chron. 28:11*ff.*). He does not hide these plans, but rather communicates them directly to his son. In addition, he collects the necessary resources to carry out his plan—talents of silver, gold, and precious stones (1 Chron. 29:1*ff.*).

The wise father invites others to help: "'Who then will offer willingly, consecrating themselves to the LORD?' Then the leaders of ancestral homes made their freewill offerings, as did also the leaders of the tribes, the commanders of the thousands and of the hundreds, and the officers over the king's work" (1 Chron. 29:5*b*-6). Their gifts are generous and everyone rejoices at the outcome. According to the Chronicler, it is the king's task to enlist others in the development of celebrations and in the completion of projects. This behavior is emphasized at every possible opportunity.

At the conclusion of David's reign, Solomon is anointed and sitting on the throne of his father David. Everyone pledges allegiance to him, with the result that "the LORD highly exalted Solomon in the sight of all Israel, and bestowed upon him such

royal majesty as had not been on any king before him in Israel"
(1 Chron. 29:25). The father's task is complete, and the son will
enjoy an even greater reputation than the father. Since the transition goes without a hitch, the desire for and execution of
vengeance (a big part of 1 Kings 1–2) disappears.

Discussion and Action

1. This chapter deals with King David's plans for the
   future. Consider what it means to plan for the future.
   Does it matter to you what happens after you are gone?
   To what extent do you consider it your responsibility to
   work for a future you will not see? What sort of future
   would you like to leave behind for those who come after
   you?

2. Review the comparisons the author makes between the
   two accounts of the transition from King David to King
   Solomon. What sorts of transitions have you taken part
   in or observed? Did they go smoothly? Why, or why
   not? What preparation was made in advance? How well
   does the church handle leadership transitions? Discuss
   how your congregation works through transitions in
   leadership.

3. Share with one another the hymns you would like sung
   at your funeral, the scriptures you would like read, and
   what you would like said about your life (see "Personal
   Preparation").

4. In the Deuteronomistic history, King David seems less
   certain and secure during the transition than in the
   Chronicler's account. How can people prepare for the
   possibility that they may be unable to make decisions
   later in life? Invite group members to share plans they
   may have put into place. What is the church's role in
   these discussions? While underscoring the importance
   of thinking about these things, respect the level at which
   various group members are willing to talk about them.

5. What parallels does Neff draw between the depictions of
   David and Moses? How significant are David's failings

in the Chronicler's and Deuteronomist's histories? These two historians also differ as to whether King David is a man of peace or man of war. To what extent are these fair or unfair characterizations? Can one's life be interpreted in conflicting ways? What sort of balance should one strike between the positive and the negative?

6. Outline some of the things that King David did in Chronicles to prepare the way for his son Solomon to build the temple. Do you think such help in general is appreciated? Explain. What did your predecessors do to help you, if anything? What are you trying to do to help others?

8

Solomon—The Wise Builder

Personal Preparation

1. Read 1 Kings 3 and 2 Chronicles 1, comparing the texts to note similarities and differences.
2. Take time to read the description of multiple intelligences at the back of the book before you go to the session. Write down which of these intelligences best describe you.
3. Try to find a musical setting for "Christ be with me." One setting can be found in *Hymnal: A Worship Book*, No. 442. The words are the eighth stanza of the Breastplate of St. Patrick.

Suggestions for Sharing and Prayer

1. Greet each other with the words, "Christ be with you." Listen to and then sing the musical setting of the Breastplate of St. Patrick called "Christ be with me."
2. This week's stanza of the Breastplate of St. Patrick describes Christ all around. (This is in contrast to last week's stanza, which described danger all around.) Assign phrases to different group members (depending on the size of the group, some may have more than one phrase), and recite the stanza, piece by piece. Discuss ways to illustrate the clauses through gesture or movement. Recite the stanza again accompanied by these movements. Pause for silent reflection. The third time through, recite the stanza using only the movements,

without any words. Pause for silence one more time. Close with spoken prayer.

3. The final clause of the prayer identifies Christ as present "in mouth of friend and stranger." How often do we identify the presence of Christ in others? What makes it easy to recognize Christ in other people? What can make it difficult? Share stories about the presence of Christ in the mouths of both friends and strangers, or about any of the other phrases in this stanza.

4. Sometimes we fail to recognize Christ in our midst because we do not always recognize different types of wisdom, knowledge, "smarts," or presence. Some educators talk about multiple intelligences, suggesting that there are many different legitimate ways of learning. Look at the list of eight kinds of learning at the back of this book. Name and claim the kinds of wisdom you think apply to you. Also name those in which you are weaker. In prayer, celebrate the overarching presence of Christ in the diversity you share as a group.

5. Close by singing again, "Christ be with me."

Understanding

Whether it's a genie granting three wishes, the mythological gods fulfilling a mortal's desire, or just plain folks sitting around a living room arguing about what they would do if they won the lottery—most of these stories are cautionary tales suggesting we be careful what we wish for. Midas nearly starved to death once everything he touched turned to gold. Many of those who win the big prize in the lottery end up more miserable than ever. And in the Bible, surely Herodias could not have been that pleased when she got her wish and was handed John the Baptist's head on a platter.

Which brings us to Solomon, and the beginning of his reign when God says he can have anything he wants. Let's back up for a minute and set the stage. The first nine chapters of 2 Chronicles are devoted to Solomon's reign. They begin with a pilgrimage to the shrine of Gibeon. Unlike the account in 1 Kings 3 where Solomon makes this pilgrimage alone, in Chronicles he is accompanied by commanders, judges, leaders, and heads of families (2 Chron. 1:2). This report echoes the behavior of David when he brings the ark to Jerusalem (1 Chron. 13:1*ff.*). The Chronicler emphasizes that the royal function in such events is to direct people to the Lord of the universe, not to themselves.

This scene is an inaugural exchange between God and the new king. God asks Solomon what gift he would most like to have (v. 7). Solomon answers, "Give me now wisdom and knowledge to go out and come in before this people, for who can rule this great people of yours?" (v. 10). God then tells Solomon that because he has this desire in his heart, he will receive riches, possessions, and honor, unparalleled by any other king in the world (v. 12). Notice that the encounter is not through an intermediary, as with David and Nathan, and not through a dream, as in 1 Kings 3:5. In Chronicles, the event is direct, face to face, much in the fashion of God's communication with Moses and in line with the aversion to dreams common in the Persian period.

What is the character of this wisdom? Wisdom can be many different things: sound judgment, artistic know-how, the capacity to make strategic plans, and the ability to define and catalog the world of nature. In 1 Kings 3, Solomon's wisdom is demonstrated in an event that follows immediately upon his return to Jerusalem. Two prostitutes ask for judgment in a dispute involving a dead child and a live child. Each claims the living child as hers. Solomon adjudicates the case by suggesting that the living child be divided in half. The real mother says to give him to the other woman. Solomon correctly discerns who the real mother is and gives her son to her. The account ends with this observation: "All Israel heard of the judgment that the king had rendered; and they stood in awe of the king, because they perceived that the wisdom of God was in him, to execute justice" (1 Kings 3:28). Wisdom is the capacity to execute sound judgment and secure justice in the realm.

This account is completely missing in Chronicles, which highlights a different kind of wisdom, namely artistic know-how: the skills of the architect, the builder, and the organizer. The Chronicler focuses on Solomon's decision to build the temple (2 Chron. 2:1). He organizes the labor and the acquisition of materials, locates the appropriate site (chapter 2); approves the architectural plans (chapter 3); and selects the furnishings, right down to the pots and pans (chapter 4). Solomon used his wisdom to provide an appropriate dwelling for the name of the Lord, since no temple could ever contain God (2 Chron. 2:5*ff.*).

In Unbroken Line

Solomon follows in the footsteps of Bezalel, the architect and designer of Israel's worship center in the wilderness. Bezazel, who designed the tent of meeting, its furnishings, and the altar at Gibeon, is described in this way: "I have filled him with divine spirit, with ability (wisdom), intelligence, and knowledge in every kind of craft, to devise artistic designs" (Exodus 31:3*ff.*). The same two Hebrew words, *chomah* (wisdom) and *da'at* (knowledge), are used in Solomon's request in 2 Chronicles 1.

Remember God's rebuke of David in 1 Chronicles 17:5: "For I have not lived in house since the day I brought out Israel to this very day, but I have lived in a tent and a tabernacle." In noting that the gifts for the creation of that meeting place are the same as those employed by Solomon in the building of the temple, the Chronicler demonstrates the continuity of the earliest worship with the present.

Just as the Chronicler places the temple in a direct line with the tabernacle, so the early Brethren, who initially worshiped in houses, modeled their first places of worship after these houses. They deliberately called them meetinghouses, not churches or cathedrals. The focus was to be on the community that met there rather than on the place. The sense of continuity for the early Brethren was also a concern for the Chronicler, although expressed in a different way.

Continuity with the past is demonstrated in other ways as well. The beginning of 2 Chronicles 5 notes that the ark, the tent of meeting, and the ancient relics are all preserved in the new edifice. The traditions of the past are utilized in the new, and the historical ties with the past are sustained. Just as the genealogy of the opening of this work carries us back to the formation of the community, the narrative of the contributions of David and Solomon takes us to the time of Moses and the creation of the tent of meeting. Sociologists tell us that when people are displaced their ties with the past, particularly family stories, are important in building stability in the present. The Chronicler writes for people who have been displaced, and provides an appropriate link to the past that is reassuring and essential for living in the postexilic age.

Where Your Treasure Is
Another major change the Chronicler makes is in the location of the description of Solomon's wealth. In 1 Kings, this accounting comes at the end of Solomon's reign, which suggests that amassing wealth is among Solomon's accomplishments (1 Kings 10:26-29). In contrast, the Chronicler locates this description at the beginning of Solomon's reign, in 2 Chronicles 1:14-17. By doing so, the Chronicler makes it explicit that such wealth is a gift of God and the fulfillment of a promise. This suggests that God followed through immediately so that Solomon might devote all of his time to building the temple. The critical historical achievement for the Chronicler is the temple, its ministries, and the way it provides the setting for worship of the one true God.

The reign of Solomon concludes with the visit of the Queen of Sheba, who tests Solomon by asking a hard question and discovers that there is nothing too difficult for him to answer (2 Chron. 9:5*ff*.). This is followed by further descriptions of Solomon's wealth and accomplishments, which confirm that the promise given by God at the beginning of this reign has been fulfilled. However, the critical gift God gave to Solomon was wisdom, which made possible a dwelling place for the Most High God.

Discussion and Action

1. What would you ask for if you were granted one wish? If someone asked you to pick out a present for yourself, how would (or did) you respond?

2. Describe the differences in the two accounts of Solomon's encounter with God. Why do you think we ended up with different stories about the same events? What reasons does Neff give?

3. What does it mean to be wise? What should be the result of wise action? Give examples of wise choices and actions you or others have made. How is Solomon's wisdom demonstrated in Kings? In Chronicles? What does this say about Solomon?

4. Educators theorize that most people have more than one sort of intelligence (see the list at the end of the book). This suggests there might be more than one way to be wise. Discuss the sorts of wisdom you believe you possess. How does this enable you to do what you do?

5. Which of these multiple intelligences do you see in what you've read of Kings and Chronicles? Which do you prefer in leaders in your community or workplace, and in your church leaders?

6. Neff states that in Chronicles Solomon asks for both wisdom and knowledge. Discuss how wisdom and knowledge are different, and how they complement each other.

7. The tabernacle and the temple represent different stages in the worship life of God's people. What are the differences between them? What are advantages and disadvantages of each? Is your church more like a tabernacle or a temple? Should church architecture say more about God or about the people who worship God within it? What does your church building say about your fellowship?

8. Solomon amassed great wealth. What rights and responsibilities go with having wealth? What, if any, are the pitfalls of too much wealth? What importance do you put on the wealth of your leaders?

9. The Queen of Sheba gives a good report of what she sees in Solomon and the kingdom. How important are the opinions of others about you and about your church? What report might your community make about your church? Would wisdom be on a list of attributes of your church?

9

The Rest of the Story

Personal Preparation

1. Read 2 Chronicles 10–12 and 29–32. Look up Hezekiah and Josiah in a Bible dictionary, on a website, or in a commentary and learn a little about them. Bring your notes to the group session.
2. Study and prepare for the *lectio divina* exercise that will be used during Sharing and Prayer time.

Suggestions for Sharing and Prayer

1. As group members settle into comfortable positions, the leader will guide the group in considering 2 Chronicles 9:23 using *lectio divina*. Explain the four steps before starting.
   - *Lectio* / Reading. The leader reads 2 Chronicles 9:23 aloud. This is a time of listening and hearing in silence.
   - *Meditatio* / Meditation. The leader shares the verse again, inviting group members to focus on one word or phrase that seems to jump out at them. In silence, group members reflect on the word or phrase, and open their hearts to the Spirit of God. The special word or phrase can be lifted up mentally, swirled around, and examined, so that associations and/or memories can cling to it. The Spirit is our guide.
   - *Oratio* / Prayer. Once again the leader reads the scripture aloud. After a minute, an individual from the group (often someone of the opposite gender from

the leader) reads the verse aloud. Again group members listen. Follow with silent or spoken prayer.

- *Contemplatio* / Contemplation. The leader reads the verse aloud for a fourth and final time. This is not a time of doing, but of resting. Be present in God. Conclude with a few moments of deep breathing, stretching, and smiling.

2. Reflect with each other on the past week. Enter into a time when hearing and listening is prayer to God. Lift up all joys, concerns, and requests silently.

3. Turn now to the ninth and final stanza of the Breastplate of St. Patrick, which is a return to the contemplation of the Trinity. Recite it aloud or sing it together as a prayer of praise. End by inviting someone to read the final stanza once again.

Understanding

When you look out the window of an airplane, it is amazing how much detail you can see right after takeoff and immediately before landing. Every window in every house is visible. When you are at a higher altitude, you can't see much detail but you have a perspective on a larger landscape.

The early chapters of this study focused on a lot of details, as will the last chapter. But in this chapter we're going to cover a lot of territory in the quest of a larger perspective on the history of God's people.

When Frank and I began this study, we had an outline in mind. However, as we began writing, the Chronicler (or the Spirit behind his work) took over, and we came to an entirely different place than where we started. An alternative story emerged, captured, and captivated us. We come to the next to last chapter of this study recognizing that there is so much more and yet so little space to articulate what the Chronicler has helped us see. This chapter encompasses 2 Chronicles 10–35, which is a significant part of the Chronicler's work. To assist in our understanding of this large body of material, we will focus on two kings—Rehoboam (chapters 10–12) and Hezekiah (chapters 29–32).

Chronicles portrays David and Solomon as ideal kings. After Solomon died, his son Rehoboam became king and things changed. Unlike his father and grandfather, Rehoboam lost touch with the people. In modern parlance, he was born inside the Beltway and no longer understood the circumstances of the people whom he governed. For example, representatives from the northern tribes asked to meet with him to talk about tax relief. He ignored these experienced leaders, opting instead to depend on courtiers without experience who had grown up with him in the palace (10:8*ff.*). He and his counselors were children of privilege, insulated from life outside Jerusalem. They had never experienced the hardships of his father and grandfather. Rehoboam responds in an insolent and arrogant manner: "My father made your yoke heavy, but I will add to it; my father disciplined you with whips, but I will discipline you with scorpions" (10:14). As a result, the ten tribes of the north revolt under the leadership of Jeroboam. This story in Chronicles closely follows the outline of 1 Kings 12:1-20.

North and South
The Deuteronomist tells the history of both north and south, but since the Chronicler does not accept the legitimacy of the northern kingdom that arises as a result of this revolt, we never hear about those kings. When Jeroboam, whose new kingdom didn't include Jerusalem with its temple, created new centers for worship and a new priesthood (2 Chron. 13:8*ff.*) the Levites and the priestly line of Aaron were forced to flee. They gave up their lands and family holdings in the north and settled in Jerusalem (2 Chron. 11:13*ff.* and 13:9*ff.*). Thus, in the Chronicler's eyes there is no legitimate worship in the north; he believes the Lord God has abandoned them.

To the Chronicler, the north has no legitimacy and thus is like any other foreign land. However, the Chronicler is quick to point out that there was always a group of loyalists in the north who maintained ties with Jerusalem (see 2 Chron. 11:16). The Chronicler insists that worship in the south received support from the north through all the years of separation. Perhaps this helps explain why the Chronicler portrays an obedient King Rehoboam during the early years of his reign, which is strikingly different from the Rehoboam portrayed in 2 Kings (Japhet 664).

The Deuteronomist and the Chronicler differ significantly in their evaluations of two other kings, Hezekiah and Josiah. For the Deuteronomist, Josiah was a key reformer who "did what was right in the sight of the LORD, and walked in all the way of his father David; he did not turn aside to the right or to the left" (2 Kings 22:2). He recovered the book of the law in the temple and structured reform around it—centralizing worship, gathering the people to read the law, cleansing the temple, and subsequently closing shop on mediums, wizards, and other idolatrous practices (2 Kings 22–23). While the Chronicler also highlights many of these reforms, in his version of the history, rather than seeming proactive, Josiah appears to merely follow what was begun by his grandfather, Hezekiah. In addition, while both histories note that Josiah gets killed in battle, only the Chronicler suggests that it was because he disobeyed God (2 Chron. 35:20-24).

A Second David

The central reformer in Chronicles is Hezekiah, who has four full chapters devoted to his reign. Raymond Dillard summarizes these three accomplishments: the reunification of Israel, the personification of the reigns of David and Solomon, and the demonstration of the reward/punishment theology of the Chronicler (228).

Hezekiah reunifies Israel. As he prepares to institute the great Passover, he sends letters not only to Judah but also to Ephraim and Manasseh (2 Chron. 30:1). The king proclaims that "from Beer-sheba to Dan . . . the people should come and keep the passover to the LORD the God of Israel, at Jerusalem" (30:5). The Chronicler's report indicates that representatives did come from Ephraim, Manasseh, Issachar, and Zebulun. This unification is made possible because during Hezekiah's reign Assyria destroyed the seat of power in the north, Samaria. The Chronicler pointedly notes that this reunification, along with the return of the people from the various territories, reflects the golden age of Solomon's era (Dillard 228).

The Chronicler puts Hezekiah into the category of David and Solomon in much the same way political parties today liken their candidates to Washington or Lincoln. In introducing Hezekiah the Chronicler says, "He did what was right in the sight of the LORD, just as his ancestor David had done" (2 Chron. 29:2). At the conclusion of the great Passover, the writer observes: "There was great joy in Jerusalem, for since the time of Solomon son of King David of Israel there had been nothing like this in Jerusalem" (2 Chron. 30:26). Two scholars, Mosis and Williams, take different sides on this question. Mosis argues that Hezekiah is the "second David" in the Chronicler's work; Williams argues that Hezekiah is a second Solomon (Dillard 229). Dillard and others take a mediating view that Hezekiah embodies both rulers, as indicated by the two passages cited from 2 Chronicles.

One of the most important theological threads of the Chronicler is immediate retribution for wrongdoing. When Hezekiah appears to take a wrong turn, he humbles himself and averts disaster (2 Chron. 32:24). He is an obedient and faithful king, and is rewarded with wealth, wisdom, and well-being (2 Chron. 32:27*ff.*). The Chronicler simply ignores the great damage Hezekiah did by taking the Babylonian spies on a tour of Jerusalem, an act that was roundly condemned by the prophet Isaiah, who informed Hezekiah that his descendents would be dragged off into captivity (2 Kings 20:12-19). The Chronicler alludes to this incident in one verse and sees it as a test but does not indicate that Hezekiah has done anything wrong (2 Chron. 32:21).

At his death, Hezekiah receives the most distinguished burial site on the ascent to the tombs of David (2 Chron. 32:33). He is the only king of whom it would be said that "all Judah and the inhabitants of Jerusalem did him honor at his death" (32:33*b*) (Japhet 997).

Discussion and Action

1. In this chapter, there is a switch from a tight focus to a larger panorama of scripture, although in Sharing and Prayer the focus is on a single verse. What are the benefits of looking at large chunks of the Bible, and also

of honing in on a very small portion? Which is more comfortable for you?

2. Rehoboam and Hezekiah present a study in contrasts, at least for the Chronicler. What are their differences? What justification can you give for Rehoboam's actions? What are Hezekiah's faults?

3. Rehoboam seems insensitive to the concerns expressed by the northern tribes. What would you have said to Rehoboam if you were an advisor? How important are listening skills to a leader? How does one determine when to listen and when to speak?

4. The Chronicler cuts out much of the story of the northern kingdom. What places in your country, state, or county do you tend to ignore? What places are more special to you than others? Can that be a blinding factor? How important is it to get to know what motivates people in other parts of the world?

5. Why do people cut off family members, fellow citizens, and fellow church members? What is the result of doing this? Why does the Chronicler seem to cut off most mention of the northern kingdom?

6. Hezekiah and Josiah are both reformers. Compare what you learned in your personal study (see "Personal Preparation") with what is expressed in 2 Chronicles. How rounded a picture does the Chronicler give? What reforms are they known for? Why was reformation necessary? What sort of reform would be useful in your church?

7. Hezekiah reunites the southern kingdom. What brokenness in your life requires reuniting? How important is it to be in unity with believers in your church, with believers in other churches, and even among other faiths?

8. Neff states that one of the most important theological threads of the Chronicler is immediate retribution for wrongdoing. When wrong is not punished, what is the effect on others? Crime dramas dominate TV and film today. Does fictional justice satisfy, at least in part, the

hunger for justice in the larger world? If so, what insight might this give to the Chronicler's viewpoint on wrong-doing and punishment?

10

The End of the Story?

Personal Preparation

1. Read 2 Chronicles 35–36 and 2 Kings 23–25. Write down a list of the kings mentioned in both histories in two columns, trying as much as possible to note overlap in their reigns.
2. Make another two-column list. In one column write the titles of books, stories, and movies with strong endings, and in the other column list titles with weak endings. Bring both lists to the session.
3. The leader should arrange for refreshments at the final session.

Suggestions for Sharing and Prayer

1. As you meet and greet each other, take some time to visit over refreshments. After a few minutes, invite reflection on this study. Talk about the study in its larger context. What have you learned? How useful has it been? What has been the most useful insight for you during this time together? Reflect also on the sharing and prayer time and its importance in your faith journeys. If this is an ongoing group, spend a few minutes talking about what you will study next.
2. Turn a final time to the Breastplate of St. Patrick. It is time to celebrate the entire prayer. Recite, sing, or chant it from start to finish. You might assign different stanzas to different people, especially if they feel a special attachment to one portion. Or you may pray in unison.

3. Step back from the prayer. Select words and phrases that have been especially meaningful to you, and lift up these lines in a spirit of prayer.
4. Review again the Prayer of Jabez found in the back of the book. Reflect on its meaning and purpose. Pray the prayer aloud in unison.
5. As your meeting winds down, take time to pray for each other, drawing upon the language of the Breastplate of St. Patrick when led to do so. If there are songs that speak more clearly to your intent, then lead the others in these songs.
6. Conclude by gathering in a circle, standing as you are able, and waiting in silence as a group, allowing yourselves to hear what God is saying. The leader may conclude with an "Amen."

Understanding

It's hard to say what is more important—the first line of a book or the last. The beginning had better be good or the reader might never get past page four. However, the ending is what leaves a lasting impression. Both Chronicles and Kings end with the same story, but they have different endings.

When we began this study, we suggested that Chronicles offers an alternate history of Israel. Through the nine previous chapters we demonstrated how this writer edited, arranged, and restructured the past. As we look at the last chapter of the book, 2 Chronicles 36, we will find that the way the story ends leads to three different conclusions as later communities understood this work. As it turns out, the end of the story is *not* the end of the story!

But before we examine these outcomes, let us look briefly at the structure of the last chapter. The Chronicler summarizes the last four kings of Judah in twenty-one verses, compared to forty-eight verses in 2 Kings 23–25. Each king is carted off into exile and pays tribute. The fall of Jerusalem at the end of Zedekiah's reign is described briefly; the Chronicler eliminates the gruesome detail of the murder of Zedekiah's sons. The Chronicler also disregards the reference in 2 Kings of the appointment of a governor after Jerusalem's destruction and the elevation of Jehoiachin. According to the Chronicler, the city is rid of all its inhabitants so the land might have sabbath rest.

The reason for the exile also changes from the long-term disobedience of the Judean kings, beginning with Manasseh in the Deuteronomistic history, to the disobedience of one king alone, Zedekiah, in Chronicles. His rebellion occurs at several levels: he did what was evil in the sight of the Lord, he did not humble himself before the prophet Jeremiah, he broke an oath sworn to God to obey Nebuchadnezzar, and he and the people polluted the house of the Lord and followed the abominations of the nations (2 Chron. 36:12-14). Although there is a hint of the continued disobedience of Judah in the Chronicler's observation that out of compassion God continually sent messengers to Judah only to be met with mockery and despising (v. 16), according to the Chronicler the reason for the final destruction rests with the reign of Zedekiah. Remember, this writer believes in immediate retribution for sin against God.

Actually the Chronicler's history of Judah ends with the action of two foreign kings. The first, the king of the Chaldeans, destroys the temple, burns down Jerusalem, kills many of its inhabitants, and carts off the rest into exile in Babylon. This ending has finality to it in 2 Kings when the writer notes that the Judean king, Jehoiachin, now sits at the Babylonian king's table (2 Kings 25:29-30). Some interpreters date this history to about 560 BCE, and from this perspective it was not clear how Judah's (Israel's) history would continue.

Of course, the Chronicler is writing almost two centuries later, and thus he can turn his attention to something completely new: the second foreign king mentioned in his account—Cyrus, the king of Persia. This king declares that "the LORD, the God of heaven, has given me all the kingdoms of the earth, and he has charged me to build him a house at Jerusalem, which is in Judah. Whoever is among you of all his people, may the LORD his God be with him! Let him go up" (2 Chron. 36:23). The

Chronicles account is mirrored in Cyrus' official records: "I returned to the sacred cities on the other side of the Tigris, the sanctuaries of which have been ruins for a long time, the images which used to live therein and established for them permanent sanctuaries. I have also gathered all their former inhabitants and returned them to their habitations" (Pritchard 316*ff.*).

The Chronicler ends his history with the official policy of a Persian king, a policy in line with the sweep of Israel's own history—namely the founding of the Lord's temple as the place of adoration and praise. What does this ending mean for future generations?

Line Up in Order
In Sunday school, you may have seen charts in which the Old Testament is divided into categories like Law, History, Prophets, Wisdom, or Poetry. The Hebrew Bible is divided more simply, into the Law (Genesis through Deuteronomy), the Prophets (former prophets, including the historical works of Joshua, Judges, 1 and 2 Samuel, and 1 and 2 Kings, and the latter prophets, including Isaiah, Jeremiah, Ezekiel, and the twelve minor prophets), and the Writings.

The earliest canonical structure in the most venerable manuscripts, Codex Leningrad and Codex Aleppo, places Chronicles first in the Writings, the third division of the Hebrew canon. This division includes 1 and 2 Chronicles, Psalms, Job, Proverbs, the Five Festal Scrolls (Song of Songs, Ruth, Ecclesiastes, Lamentations, and Esther), Daniel, Ezra, and Nehemiah. One way to explain this position for Chronicles lies in its focus on the worship life of Israel. Chronicles focuses the history of Israel in its devotional life, centering this activity on the reigns of David and Solomon, who introduced music, thus providing an appropriate introduction to the Psalter. Chronicles introduces the liturgical life of Israel.

However, when the Septuagint was organized, Chronicles was understood primarily as a historical work related to the books of Samuel and Kings, so it was placed in between them and Ezra and Nehemiah. In fact, it is linked directly to what follows by the repetition of the last two verses of 2 Chronicles 36 at the beginning of Ezra 1. Such placement made perfect sense, since in this position it prepared the way for the restoration of Jerusalem and the rebuilding of the temple that is described in Ezra and Nehemiah. This close association led a number of late nineteenth- to early twentieth-century scholars to consider that these works belonged together and had a common author. Protestant Bibles follow the Septuagint's arrangement of the historical works.

The Last Shall Be—Next
The third structure follows the Babylonian canon and can be found in the current Hebrew Bible used by Jews today. In this structure, 1 and 2 Chronicles come last. This order was adopted by the Council of Jamnia in 90 CE, 20 years after the destruction of Jerusalem and the temple in 70 CE, making the last verse of Chronicles the final verse of the Hebrew Bible. Rebuilding the temple is a job that remains—and there is a mandate for that job from Cyrus!

Compare that to the Protestant Bible, which ends with Malachi: "Lo, I will send you the prophet Elijah before the great and terrible day of the LORD comes. He will turn the hearts of parents to their children" (4:5-6). The Synoptic tradition takes these verses as reference to John the Baptist, who signifies the coming of the Messianic age. The very structure of the Protestant Bible points Christians toward the return of the Messiah.

Each of these works looks beyond itself. No better place is that expressed than in the book of Chronicles, which invites us into an alternative story and to think about alternative endings, endings that include hope and vision for the future. This ending is really a beginning that demands we put ourselves in the story. And we are not only to put ourselves in the story, but to help write the next chapter.

Discussion and Action
   1. Referring to the lists you made (see "Personal Preparation"), discuss the importance of strong beginnings and

endings in books, stories, and movies. Share some examples. Compare the endings of 2 Kings and 2 Chronicles. In light of your reading of these texts and your reading of the study guide, which book has the stronger ending? Which is more hopeful? Why?

2. The question of swift retribution comes up again at the end of 2 Chronicles. What are your thoughts about this? Why do you think this is not as much of a concern for the writer of Kings?

3. The Chronicler speaks of the land having rest. What does this mean? Discuss whether you view creation as a character, and the things of this world as having personality. Is rest necessary for the land? If so, why?

4. Discuss the three placements of Chronicles in the Bible. What is the significance of each of these different placements?

5. This study explores the way two biblical historians look at the same history differently. What are your thoughts now, at the end of the study, regarding alternate views of history? Is it legitimate to look at events in different ways? Is the premise of this book on track, or mistaken? What insights have you gained into the way biblical writers operated? What does this say about the nature of inspiration? Is what you're learning comforting, or is it disconcerting, and why?

6. Many felt that the carnage of the American Civil War was inevitable because of the sins of slavery. Reflect on the two biblical views of the fall of Jerusalem as punishment for sin, and discuss whether it was inevitable. In what ways do nations and individuals suffer for wrongdoing? What is the place of repentance in relationships among nations?

7. The Chronicler makes the astonishing assertion that the nonbeliever Cyrus is an agent of God. Does God work through nonbelievers and people of other faiths for the kingdom today? And if so, how?

8. To what extent is the commission at the end of
   Chronicles to go and build the temple valid today? Does
   an open-ended mission invite people to action, or does it
   tire them? Share personal or congregational stories of
   both responses.

Resource Pages

St. Patrick's Breastplate

Very little is known about the fifth-century evangelist St. Patrick, who is thought to have preached in Ireland. This prayer poem attributed to him dates back at least to the eighth century. It has been translated from the Old Irish into many languages.

1. I bind unto myself today
   The strong Name of the Trinity,
   By invocation of the same,
   The Three in One and One in Three.

2. I bind this day to me for ever,
   By pow'r of faith, Christ's Incarnation;
   His baptism in Jordan River;
   His death on Cross for my salvation;
   His bursting from the spiced tomb;
   His riding up the Heav'nly way;
   His coming at the day of doom;
   I bind unto myself to-day.

3. I bind unto myself the power
   Of the great love of Cherubim;
   The sweet "Well done" in judgment hour;
   The service of the Seraphim,
   Confessors' faith, Apostles' word,
   The Patriarchs' prayers, the Prophets' scrolls,
   All good deeds done unto the Lord,
   And purity of virgin souls.

4. I bind unto myself to-day
   The virtues of the star-lit heaven,
   The glorious sun's life-giving ray,
   The whiteness of the moon at even,

The flashing of the lightning free,
The whirling wind's tempestuous shocks,
The stable earth, the deep salt sea,
Around the old eternal rocks.

5. I bind unto myself to-day
The pow'r of God to hold, and lead,
His eye to watch, His might to stay,
His ear to hearken to my need.
The wisdom of my God to teach,
His hand to guide, His shield to ward;
The word of God to give me speech,
His heavenly host to be my guard.

6. Against the demon snares of sin,
The vice that gives temptation force,
The natural lusts that war within,
The hostile men that mar my course;
Or few or many, far or nigh,
In every place, and in all hours,
Against their fierce hostility,
I bind to me these holy powers.

7. Against all Satan's spells and wiles,
Against false words of heresy,
Against the knowledge that defiles,
Against the heart's idolatry,
Against the wizard's evil craft,
Against the death-wound and the burning,
The choking wave, the poison'd shaft,
Protect me, Christ, till Thy returning.

8. Christ be with me, Christ within me,
Christ behind me, Christ before me,
Christ beside me, Christ to win me,
Christ to comfort and restore me,

Christ beneath me, Christ above me,
Christ in quiet, Christ in danger,
Christ in hearts of all that love me,
Christ in mouth of friend and stranger.

9. I bind unto myself the Name,
    The strong Name of the Trinity;
    By invocation of the same,
    The Three in One, and One in Three.
    Of Whom all nature hath creation:
    Eternal Father, Spirit, Word:
    Praise to the Lord of my salvation,
    Salvation is of Christ the Lord.

From *Poems* by Cecil Frances Alexander, New York: The MacMillan Company, 1897, pp. 59-62. Translated for the *Irish Church Hymnal*. Used as a processional in York Minster at the enthronement of William C. Magee, Archbishop of York.

The Prayer of Jabez (1 Chron. 4:10)

"Oh that thou wouldest bless me indeed, and enlarge my coast, and that thine hand might be with me, and that thou wouldest keep me from evil, that it may not grieve me!" (King James Version)

"Oh that thou wouldst bless me and enlarge my border, and that thy hand might be with me, and that thou wouldst keep me from harm so that it might not hurt me!" (Revised Standard Version)

"Oh that you would bless me and enlarge my border, and that your hand might be with me, and that you would keep me from hurt and harm!" (New Revised Standard Version)

"Oh, that You would bless me indeed, and enlarge my territory, that Your hand would be with me, and that You would keep *me* from evil, that I may not cause pain!" (New King James Version)

"Bless me, O bless me! Give me land, large tracts of land. And provide your personal protection—don't let evil hurt me." (The Message)

"Oh, bless me, enlarge my territory, stand by me, and make me not suffer pain from misfortune!" (Jewish Publication Society)

"Oh, that you would bless me and enlarge my territory! Let your hand be with me, and keep me from harm so that I will be free from pain." (New International Version)

Multiple Intelligences

Some educators talk about theory of multiple intelligences. In other words, there are many different legitimate ways of learning. These are not restrictive labels intended to box people into categories, but observations that can give insight as to why some things come easier to some and with more difficulty to others. Typically, individuals can lay claim to several of these. Eight multiple intelligences are commonly identified, but others describe more or less. A high school principal described these eight types of intelligence as "eight ways of being smart," and pointed out that educators need to take all of these into account when working with students.

Bodily-Kinesthetic people learn best by doing. They like movement, have a good sense of balance and eye-hand coordination, and are good at physical activities like sports, dance, performance, and plays.

Interpersonal learners are extroverts who learn better in company of others. They work well in groups, enjoy discussion and debate, and make both good followers and leaders.

Mathematical-Logical people are strong in logic and abstraction. They can see patterns, ask questions, are curious, are good at experiments, and have mathematical skills.

Naturalistic intelligence is associated with nurturing, nature, and sensitivity to natural surroundings. These people learn best in nature, and are good at collecting, cataloging, and categorizing.

Verbal-Linguistic people learn by reading, through discussion, and taking notes. They are good listeners and good speakers. They memorize, and are good at explaining.

Visual-Spatial intelligence involves the artistic bent. These people learn by visualizing and through puzzles. They create vivid mental images, think in pictures, and enjoy touch.

Intrapersonal learners are introverts who learn on their own. They are reflective, have a strong self-awareness, can concentrate for long periods, and make good philosophers.

Musical people are, of course, musical. They learn well by lecture, have a strong sense of rhythm, like to sing, play instruments, sometimes have perfect pitch, and may compose music.

Bibliography

Bass, Diana Butler. *A People's History of Christianity: The Other Side of the Story.* New York: HarperCollins, 2009.

Braun, Roddy. *1 Chronicles.* Word Biblical Commentary, vol. 14. Waco: Word Books, 1986.

Childs, Brevard S. *Introduction to the Old Testament as Scripture.* Philadelphia: Fortress Press, 1979.

Dillard, Raymond B. *2 Chronicles.* Word Biblical Commentary, vol. 15. Waco: Word Books, 1988.

Japhet, Sara. *I and II Chronicles: A Commentary.* The Old Testament Library. Louisville: Westminster John Knox, 1993.

Myers, Jacob M. *I Chronicles.* The Anchor Bible. Garden City, N.Y.: Doubleday and Co., 1965.

Myers, Jacob M. *II Chronicles.* The Anchor Bible. Garden City, N.Y.: Doubleday and Co., 1965.

Pritchard, James Bennett, ed. *Ancient Near Eastern Texts Relating to the Old Testament.* Princeton, N.J.: Princeton University Press, 1969.

Schweitzer, Steven. *Reading Utopia in Chronicles.* The Library of Hebrew Bible/Old Testament Studies, vol. 442. London: T & T Clark International, 2007.

Other Covenant Bible Studies

Each book is $7.95 plus shipping and handling. For a full description of each title, ask for a free catalog of these and other Brethren Press titles. Major credit cards accepted. Prices subject to change.

Regular Customer Service hours are Monday through Friday, 8:30 a.m. to 5:30 p.m. CDT.

Brethren Press • 1451 Dundee Avenue • Elgin, Illinois 60120
Phone: 800-441-3712 • Fax: 800-667-8188
e-mail: brethrenpress@brethren.org
www.brethrenpress.com